D1507997

LATINO
LITERATURE
IN AMERICA

LATINO
LITERATURE
IN AMERICA

Bridget Kevane

Literature as Windows to World Cultures

GREENWOOD PRESS
Westport, Connecticut • London

Library of Congress Cataloging-in-Publication Data

Kevane, Bridget A., 1963–
    Latino literature in America / by Bridget Kevane.
        p. cm. — (Literature as windows to world cultures, ISSN 1543–9968)
    Includes bibliographical references (p.   ) and index.
    ISBN 0–313–31793–3 (alk. paper)
    1. American literature—Hispanic American authors—History and criticism.
  2. Hispanic Americans—Intellectual life. 3. Hispanic Americans in literature.
  I. Title. II. Series
        PS153.H56K48   2003
        810.9′868—dc21   2003048526

British Library Cataloguing in Publication Data is available.

Copyright © 2003 by Bridget Kevane

Library of Congress Catalog Card Number: 2003048526
ISBN: 0–313–31793–3
ISSN: 1543–9968

First published in 2003

Greenwood Press, 88 Post Road West, Westport, CT 06881
An imprint of Greenwood Publishing Group, Inc.
www.greenwood.com

Printed in the United States of America

The paper used in this book complies with the
Permanent Paper Standard issued by the National
Information Standards Organization (Z39.48–1984).

10   9   8   7   6   5   4   3   2   1

Contents

Introduction

Literature, as critic Stephen Greenblatt says, stands as an important "creature and a creator of culture." This book is an effort to capture different Latino cultures through the literature of the eight authors included here. The reader can discover Latino communities and their culture across the United States by reading the literary production emerging from Latino communities. Autobiography, poetry, novels, short stories, and essays of Latino literature provide a detailed slice of life that can sometimes be radically different from the reader's own world. Literature is one of those unique forms of cultural production that allows the individual to travel without leaving the confines of his or her home, and a social record that marks different periods, issues, conflicts, and celebrations of any given person or peoples. Without literature, we would not have such a record from which to learn.

Each novel contains infinite possibilities that segue into cultural aspects students might enjoy exploring. The Trujillo dictatorship, the Mexican-American War, the Castro revolution, Spanish Harlem, Little Havana, Washington Heights, *la frontera*, the Nuyorican Poets' Cafe, *espiritismo*, *santería*, *curanderas*, *la Virgen de Guadalupe*, *La Llorona*, mambo and salsa, Spanish and Spanglish. Ideas about history, religion, music, cultural myths, geographical spaces, and politics are all found in these novels that offer many themes for students to investigate. Opportunities for compare and contrast papers abound. One can compare and contrast the Virgin Mary with *la Virgen de Guadalupe*, or the portrayal of *la Virgen* in the works of Anaya versus that in the works of Cisneros, who plays with the passive yet forgiving *Virgen*. Other possibilities are *Santería* versus *curanderismo,* the urban landscape of Spanish Harlem versus that of Nuevo Mexico. Students can discover rich cultural elements that they might pursue beyond the novel for class presentations, final papers, or cultural capsules. Most importantly, readers will be able to relate to these works because the common denominator of the literature in this volume is the journey toward a better understanding of one's identity, culture, history, past, and future. Whatever kind of journey the characters and/or authors have undertaken, students will be able to find parallels with their own journeys toward their identity, their roots, and their cultures.

What does it mean to be a Latino in the United States? Who are Latinos? Who are Chicanos, Nuevo Mexicanos, Cubanos, Nuyoricans, Puerto Ricans, Boricuas, Dominicanos, Quisqueyanos, Mexicano Americanos?[1] What is Latino culture? How do Latinos think and feel, and what would they say if asked about their culture and history? Answers to these questions about Latino culture can be found in the fiction of the eight authors discussed here: the Dominican Americans Julia Alvarez and Junot Díaz, the Chicanos Rudolfo Anaya and Sandra Cisneros, the Cuban Americans Cristina García and Oscar Hijuelos, and the *puertorriqueños* Judith Ortiz Cofer and Ernesto Quiñonez. All of these authors maintain ties to their Spanish cultural and linguistic heritage, which includes that of Cuba, the Dominican Republic, Puerto Rico, and Mexico. Their novels and stories invite readers to explore and learn about Latino culture and, at the same time, to transcend cultural differences in order to better understand and accept the Latino communities found across the United States.

Culture is human expression. It encompasses large systems in which communities remain linked and organized, such as language, history, religion, mythology, traditions, geography, and gender roles. Culture also expresses the unique habits of communities passed down from generation to generation, such as food, dress, festivals, art, literature, and music. For marginalized communities, culture takes on a further and, at times, more urgent meaning: culture functions as a survival mechanism and a way of expressing political power. It is a survival mechanism in that it creates a sense of collective self-respect and of resistance vis-à-vis the dominant culture. In the sixties, for example, Chicanos and Puerto Ricans joined the Civil Rights Movement in an attempt to foster pride in their people and to find political empowerment.

Culture is not a static system of customs or traditions, but rather a fluid interaction of elements that merge, change, and evolve. As communities pass through dictatorships, exile, poverty, and immigration, like those portrayed in the fiction included here—as they seek survival and a better quality of life in the United States—their cultures inevitably evolve, adapting and adopting, discarding and eliminating traditions of the past, while creating new ones for the future. The literature analyzed in this volume stands as testament to the dynamic interaction of cultural elements: just as cultures are fluid, so too is the interaction between the individual and his or her culture. For example, the Chicana writer Sandra Cisneros reinvents *la Virgen de Guadalupe* as a powerful goddess instead of the traditional passive and unselfish Virgin, whereas the Chicano Rudolfo Anaya portrays *la Virgen* in her more traditional role. Puerto Rico as the homeland has a radically different meaning for Ernesto Quiñonez than it does for Puerto Rican Judith Ortiz Cofer. Further, as the authors grow as spokespeople for their cultures, they reassess, adopt, discard, and change their perceptions and habits with regard to their culture and their homeland. If at first Alvarez wanted to convey the cultural conflict inherent in being Dominican and American, she slowly moved toward relaying the historical and national conflict of her country. Whatever the relationship the authors maintain to their cultures, what remains fundamental in their work is the need to preserve and communicate their particular culture to their readers.

Given the diversity present in the eleven works of fiction in this volume, I will not address the same cultural elements in every text, but rather focus on the most important cultural feature that the author deals with in his or her work. For example, although I address in depth the syncretic African/Puerto Rican folk religion of *santería* and *espiritismo* in Ortiz Cofer's novel, I do not emphasize it in Díaz's or Quiñonez's novels, even though it is present in their works as well. Gender issues as they relate to women are predominant in Cisneros's work, although they appear in García's work as well. In addition, several times I will cross reference themes found in works suggesting the possibilities for comparisons. The culture of *barrio* poverty, and its resulting issues of shame and invisibility, is prevalent in the works of Sandra Cisneros, Junot Díaz, and Ernesto Quiñonez. Coming-of-age novels characterize the works of Cisneros, Anaya, and Ortiz Cofer. Other works, like that of Quiñonez, García, and Díaz, reflect a more jaded coming-of-age, as their characters are transformed later in life. The attempt to return to the homeland, the islands, or Mexico is seen in several works as well, but takes center stage in Alvarez's *How the García Girls Lost Their Accents*. All of the themes portrayed in these novels attest to the growing and interactive role of Latino culture in mainland North America. The final goal of this book is to convey to readers the variety and richness of the Latino cultures from Georgia to New Mexico, from Spanish Harlem to Chicago, from Habana to Santo Domingo.

HISTORICAL BACKGROUND

The Homelands

Despite the fact that some of the authors have never lived in or visited their homelands, the homeland informs their work at a social, cultural, political, and historical level. The homelands represented in this book contain a rich cultural and ethnic history with which the reader should become familiar in order to best understand the fiction of the Latino writers included here. The Spanish-speaking islands of Cuba, formerly known as *Ciboney;* the Dominican Republic, known as *Quisqueya;* and Puerto Rico, whose native name was *Borínquen,* had Arawak, Taíno, Carib, and other smaller indigenous populations. These populations developed art, music, and languages unique to them. Mexico, in turn, had advanced civilizations, the most well-known being the Aztec and Mayan empires. With the arrival of the Spanish conquistadors in 1492, and the subsequent colonization of these countries, the mixing of races became inevitable. Today in Mexico, for example, roughly 60 percent of the population is *mestizo* (Amerindian and Spanish), while about 30 percent are descendants of the native populations. On the islands, the *mestizaje* consists mostly of the interracial mixing between Africans and Spaniards, as the indigenous populations were decimated and then replaced with African slaves. The culture and traditions of the African slaves have found their way into contemporary island cultures, especially in religious and spiritual matters in Cuba, the Dominican Republic, and Puerto Rico. In fact, it would be impossible to understand *santería* without knowing something of the Western African Yoruban slaves and their religious practices like Orisha, which formed the basis for *santería. Santería,* a folk religion prevalent in the Spanish Caribbean where slaves were predominant, combines African gods with Catholic saints. It continues to be a part of the literature by Latinos from the islands, both on the mainland and on the islands themselves. In addition, musical rhythms from the Western African slaves had their influence on the mambo, rumba, merengue, and salsa of Cuba, the Dominican Republic, and Puerto Rico, a theme in the fiction of Hijuelos and Quiñonez.

The Spanish Caribbean islands and Mexico became colonies of Spain for roughly 500 years. Throughout Spanish rule, the countries sought independence. But it was not until the nineteenth century that the countries emerged as modern nations. Mexico's struggle for independence began in 1810 with the *Grito de Hidalgo* (named after the priest Miguel de Hidalgo, who organized the call to independence), and ended in 1821. Cuba and Puerto Rico's struggles began in the 1860s but did not end until 1898 with the War of 1898. Although little mention is made of Spanish rule in the novels included here, both Anaya, Alvarez, and García trace their characters' ancestors back to Spain and to a long line of conquistadors. The Dominican Republic had a different history since Spanish rule there began faltering in the seventeenth century. For almost a century the island was fought over by the French, Dutch, British, and Spanish powers until it became part of Haiti, from which it finally gained independence in 1844.

Although each of these countries achieved independence in the nineteenth century, their emergence as autonomous nations was thwarted and complicated in different ways by the United States. The Monroe Doctrine of 1823 stood as a warning to European powers to stay out of the hemisphere (Coerver and Hall 4). Manifest Destiny was used to defend the War of 1846–48 between Mexico and the United States and allowed for the annexation of the Southern United States. The War of 1898, typically known as the Spanish-American War, consolidated United States control in the Caribbean. Years later, the Good Neighbor Policy formed by Franklin Delano Roosevelt would maintain United States authority on the islands.

The war between Mexico and the United States began over the rebellious territory of Texas, which the United States annexed in 1845. Although formally under Mexican rule, the United States, with Mexico's approval, began settling the territory. Soon, however, Mexico found itself embroiled in a war with the United States, as Texans, and even Tejanos, those of Mexican descent, wanted annexation to the United States. During the rule of the President of Mexico, Antonio López de Santa Anna, the United States invaded Mexico and the defiant state of Texas with the goal of shifting the border between Mexico and the United States. The war, won by the United States, resulted in the Treaty of Guadalupe Hidalgo, signed in 1848 in the city of that name. Santa Anna ceded 55 percent of Mexico's territory, most of what is today Arizona, California, New Mexico, Texas, and parts of Colorado, Nevada, and Utah. They received, in exchange, $15 million. Mexico was allowed to retain everything south of the Rio Grande or, as Mexicans called it, the Río Bravo. What was formerly known as *El Norte de México* (Northern Mexico), now became the American Southwest.

The treaty stated that it would protect land that already belonged to those living there and the owners' civil rights. But, this promise was not well protected. Mexican citizens who had lived in the north, *tejanos, californios, nuevo mexicanos,* and others who desired to remain under Mexican rule had to move south. Still others, either unable to uproot or feeling strongly that their heritage was tied to their land, remained. Those who remained were forced to give up their Mexican identity and to become American citizens. If they did not comply, they had to return to southern Mexico, a place as foreign to them as another country. Modern Chicano history continues to emphasize the long history Mexicans have had in the United States, both under Mexican and then United States rule.

On April 19, 1898, Spain and the United States declared war against each other over Cuba and the Philippines. The United States won the war and received Puerto Rico as war booty. Under the Treaty of Paris, Puerto Rico was annexed by the United States, and the people of Puerto Rico received United States citizenship in 1917 with the Jones Act. Today, Puerto Rico is a commonwealth, an *estado libre asociado,* a free associated state. Cuba, in turn, became independent but with certain constraints placed upon it by the United States. Under the Platt Amendment, signed in 1901, the "United States reserves and retains the right of intervention for the preservation of Cuban independence and the maintenance of a stable government" (Pérez, Jr. 186). The agreement also granted the United States Guantánamo Bay, which it still holds today. As the foundering Dominican Republic experienced unstable years of political chaos, the United States agreed to manage the island's economic debts. By 1911, the United States had become heavily involved in island politics, finally occupying the island from 1916–1924.

Dictatorships emerged in the Dominican Republic and Cuba that led to much of the emigration and exile of its citizens. Rafael Leonidas Molina de Trujillo ruled the Dominican Republic from 1930–1961, and Fulgencio Batista, 1933–1944, 1952–59, and Fidel Castro, 1959–present, have ruled Cuba. Although the repressions of the Trujillo dictatorship drove Dominicans to the United States, after his assassination Dominicans kept emigrating in search of more political and economic stability. The United States, in fact, occupied the Dominican Republic again in 1965, an event described by both Alvarez and Díaz in their fiction, which led to further ties between the two countries. Although many Dominicans fled first Trujillo, then Joaquín Balaguer, today the poverty that persists on the island drives Dominicans to seek a better life in the United States. Junot Díaz's story "Negocios" underscores this emigration. There are today an estimated half million Dominicans in the tri-state area of New Jersey, New York, and Connecticut.

The establishment of Castro, and the subsequent United States embargo against the Cuban government, has led to a series of major migrations by Cubans, as described in Cristina García's novels. Puerto Ricans, in turn, arrived in their greatest numbers during the fifties, called the Great Migration, when the United States and the island reached an agreement titled Operation Bootstrap. There are roughly 2.5 million Puerto Ricans on the mainland today. Mexico's economy and borders have long been porous. The United States illegally employs thousands of Mexicans, termed *braceros* (brazers) because they provide cheap farm labor, especially in the West. The latest U.S. Census Bureau reported that legal Mexicans reflect almost 30 percent of the populations of many of the states in the Southwest (California, Texas, Arizona, New Mexico), and almost 13 percent of the total North American population. It is not clear how many of these are working illegally. The political stance toward these illegals, as well as border control, continue to be fiercely debated and contribute to derogatory stereotypes on both sides of the border.

The Second Homeland

Latino communities have existed in the United States since the nineteenth century. Many Puerto Ricans and Cubans, for example, funded and organized their struggle for independence from Spanish rule while living on the mainland. Mexicans, previously known as *californios, tejanos,* or *nuevo mexicanos,* for example, have lived on the mainland since Mexico's independence in 1821. Despite their long history on the mainland, it wasn't until the Civil Rights Movement that Latinos as a political and social entity exploded across the mainland. Latino activists and militant political groups emerged during the sixties, groups like the Young Lords, La Raza Unida/The United People, the Brown Berets, and the Cuban Brothers in Exile. These groups generally shunned their "adopted" homeland and eternally spoke of the return home as the only dignified solution for their own communities.

One of the forerunners of Mexican Chicano activism in the sixties was César Chavez, who began the United Farm Workers' Union, and generated a defining moment in the creation of a new social and political consciousness among Mexicans in the United States. He organized and led massive strikes against large grape and farm companies. In fact, as a result of his activism, Mexicans who were politically active adopted the name Chicano, a derivative of Mexicanos (xicanos; the 'x' pronounced as an 'sh'), that was originally derogatory and directed at poor immigrant laborers. Chicanos in New Mexico even attempted to reclaim their land lost in the war of 1846–48. From Chavez's militant activism many organizations emerged, such as *La Raza* or *Mecha* (Movimiento Estudiantil Chicano de Aztlán), a student movement that continues to this day. It promotes Chicanos' Mexican roots, social awareness, and political empowerment. In 1969, *El Plan Espiritual de Aztlán* (The Plan of Aztlan) was written at the first Chicano National Conference. A Chicano political manifesto, the plan characterized the political and ideological beliefs of Chicanos and emphasized nationalism and self-determination. At the same time, Puerto Ricans mobilized on the East Coast. One of the most important organizations to shape a new future for Puerto Ricans was named the Young Lords Party. This organization sought to mobilize Puerto Ricans and Latinos across the mainland through their 13-Point Plan, described in Quiñonez's novel, which called for freeing Latinos from oppression and Puerto Rico from "colonialism."

Literary Traditions

Although the literature addressed in this book is contemporary, the oldest text being that of Rudolfo A. Anaya (1972), the reader should know that the Hispanic literary tradition began much earlier. There was literary production, for example, north of the Rio Grande even before the United States was founded: "Hispanic literature, a literature created by the people proudly emerging from the fusion of Spanish, Native American, and African cultures, has always been part of the mosaic of the United States" (Kanellos 1–2).

During the late sixties and the seventies small presses began to publish the work of the silenced voices of Latinos across the country. In the seventies, Tomás Rivera's *Y no se lo tragó la tierra . . . / And the Earth Did Not Devour Him* (1970), Anaya's *Bless Me, Ultima* (1972), and José Antonio Villarreal's *Pocho* (1970), all considered classics, were published. In the eighties, Chicana women responded by publishing literature with a definite feminist slant, targeting patriarchal oppression and redefining the traditional Mexican woman. Chicana writers like Sandra Cisneros, Cherríe Moraga, Gloria Anzaldúa, Ana Castillo, and Helena María Viramontes began publishing poetry, stories, and autobiographical pieces that gave voice to Chicana women across the country. The Puerto Rican literary scene also began to flourish in the sixties and seventies with the establishment of the Nuyorican Poets' Café in New York City and writers like Pedro Pietri, Piri Thomas, Pedro Juan Soto, and Miguel Piñero, who received praise and recognition from mainstream literary establishments. Nicholasa Mohr is considered a pioneer in Puerto Rican writing in English done by a woman, and has been followed by Judith Ortiz Cofer and Esmeralda Santiago. A younger generation of Puerto Rican male writers includes Abraham Rodríguez, Jr. and Ernesto Quiñonez, included in this volume. Cuban American literature emerged in the eighties with Oscar Hijuelos, Gustavo Pérez Firmat and, more recently, Cristina García, Yvonne Lamazares, Ana Menendez, Beatriz Rivera, and Ana Veciana-Suarez. Dominican writers remain the newest literary group of writers. Junot Díaz, included here, Loida Maritza Perez, Angie Cruz, and Nelly Rosario have all been published in the late nineties and early 2000s.

Today, there exists a body of Latino literature that spans almost four decades. The works that cover these decades reveal writers engaged in an ongoing dialogue with their cultures. History, gender, language, and more are addressed by all of the Latino writers mentioned above in distinct ways. These authors are forcing North American readers to recognize their presence not only on a political level but on a cultural level. One small example of the growing importance of Latinos politically is the fact that both presidential candidates in the 1999 election primaries addressed Latino communities in Spanish. Many of the novels included in this volume contain Spanish in their narratives. Spanish, as reporter Juan Gonzalez points out, "is not a foreign tongue in the United States. It is the principal language of the Western Hemisphere and the second language of the United States, and should finally be recognized as such" (272). In the end, the small selection of writers included here represent different views of their cultures and their interaction with the North American culture.

THE LATINO IDENTITY

Much of the terminology used by critics, readers, and writers describes the sense of displacement that reveals what it feels like to be Latino: a hybrid, bilingual, bicultural individual who is sharing two worlds, straddling the fence, belonging neither here nor there, belonging both here and there, being from two worlds, living in the borderlands, living on the hyphen, being a gringoriqueño, a Dominican American, a Dominican York, a gringa Dominican, a nuyorican, a neorican, a Chicano, a mexicano americano. Typically, Latinos who describe the sensation of belonging to two worlds are seen as acculturated since they do not abandon their Latino heritage, nor do they reject North American culture. They adopt elements from both cultures. At the same time, there are many Latinos who are proud to be Americans, who are fully assimilated and simply call themselves Americans. There are also those Latinos who are militant in their anti-American feelings, as were many radicals of the sixties, and who see the return to the homeland as the only possible solution for them. These Latinos can be described as underacculturated since they have rejected North American culture. What stands out in the fiction included here is that all of the authors and their characters find a final resolution in the act of adopting both cultures, in becoming bicultural.

The scope of this series is to focus on a geographical area of the world which has produced a body of literature reflecting the cultural concerns of that area. There is nothing more unique than that body of literature that either defies or transcends the geographical area, as do Latino/Latina literatures. One of the difficulties in defining this geographical area is its connections and political relationships to the United States. Cuba, Puerto Rico, the Dominican Republic, and the Southwest Mexican homeland, have almost arbitrary, flexible, and permeable borders. Where do we situate the cultural context of, for example, Sandra Cisneros or Julia Alvarez? Is Hijuelo's work informed by New York or Cuba? Does it reflect the culture of New York or Cuba? The answer lies in what is becoming more and more apparent: borders are fluid. Some are tangible, like bridges, gates, and rivers and are crossed by foot, plane, or boat. But, others are not tangible. In the particular case of American Latino literature, the United States may be the writer's new home, whereas the Latino/Latina emphasizes his or her Hispanic heritage. The geographical area moves, as do the authors, from New York to Puerto Rico, from Chicago to Mexico, from Miami to Cuba, or back and forth and in between.

One element that characterizes the doubleness of the authors or of their characters' identities is the fact that most Latinos can claim two homelands. In this sense, landscape, a sense of place, is an imperative element of these authors' works. It describes their origin and how it remains a part of their

identity. Latino authors draw both internal and external boundaries for
Latinos living in the United States. If the reader were to draw a map of the
United States and the Caribbean and locate the geographical locations of
these authors, the locations would span quite a distance, from their places of
origin to their new homelands. From Anaya's small towns of New Mexico
to García's trips to and from Habana and Miami; from Alvarez's town of
Burlington, Vermont, to her characters' home in New York and back to the
town of Cibao in the Dominican Republic; from Díaz's *campo* in Santo
Domingo to Washington Heights, all of the authors draw on their urban
and rural landscapes to emphasize how the sense of place affects the individual. Several of the authors represented here were born in their country of
origin: Cristina García in Cuba, Judith Ortiz Cofer in Puerto Rico, Junot
Díaz in the Dominican Republic. Others, like Julia Alvarez, Oscar Hijuelos,
Sandra Cisneros, and Rudolfo Anaya were born in the United States.
Ernesto Quiñonez was born in Ecuador, but his family came to New York
when he was a year and a half old. Alvarez returned to Santo Domingo
almost immediately after she was born. This migration to and from and
between mainland and island attests to the bicultural nature of these
authors. Quiñonez represents an even further hybrid of a new Latino, born
out of the interactions between Latinos, who married outside of one ethnic
race (Ecuador and Puerto Rico). Despite, or because of, their place of birth,
all of the authors maintain connections through their parents or grandparents, through extended family, to the language and to the customs of their
homelands.

For exiles or immigrants, arrival to the mainland can be shocking either
because of the poverty they have left behind or the political restraints of a
dictatorship. In this respect, their sense of place is shaped on the mainland
as they confront the liberties and, at times, excesses of the United States, in
addition to the struggles of living there. A dictatorship tears apart not only
physical homes and nations, but the very identities of individuals. Trujillo
and Castro trampled on their citizens; confiscated their lands; and stripped
the people of their rights, of justice, of the power to defend themselves, and
the power to speak out against the violations. For those escaping dictatorships, like the one portrayed in Alvarez's and García's novels, the shock
might relate to the freedom of speech, the freedom to criticize anything
and everything—to take a stance against the President, to create political
cartoons, to engage in activities that under the Trujillo and Castro regimes
would most likely have sent them to jail and death. Habits of caution born
from dictatorships become lifelong habits. For the father of the García girls,
irreverence toward authority is perceived with fear. Daily elements are also
different, from courtship to education, from gender roles to eating habits.
In both Alvarez's and Díaz's work, the older generation of arriving immigrants are amazed by the abundance and extravagance of the "American
way of life," the freedom and liberties. For the exile or immigrant, adjust-

ing to the American way of life is a series of shocks and revelations that vacillate between old and new world traditions. If in some novels discussed in this book, like those of Alvarez and García, we saw cultures emerge under dictatorships or in exile, in Cisneros's, Díaz's, and Quiñonez's work, we read about cultures living in the United States. These are the cultures created in *barrios* and in segregated neighborhoods. When the characters emerge outside the boundaries of their neighborhoods, they understand the economic disparity and inherent racism that keeps them segregated from mainstream America.

One of the greater cultural issues in all of the works presented here is that of the disparity between the homeland and the new home, and a coming-of-age within this cultural struggle. In most of the novels, the homeland represents the traditional patriarchal Spanish-style world. The conflict between the two worlds manifests itself principally in gender roles. Machismo and submissive Latina women are portrayed in the stories and novels that attempt to break these stereotypes. " 'Macho' is the accepted—and expected—single-word description synonymous with Latino men and male culture" (Rivera 502). César Castillo is the epitome of the macho Cuban. In turn, the Latina is supposed to be submissive, passive, and domestic, to model herself on the traditional *Virgen*. In Cisneros's work, the women are supposed to emulate *la Virgen*. The characters in *Woman Hollering Creek* fiercely defend themselves against this submissive and passive role model, and instead empower *la Virgen* with the ancient Aztec goddess Coatlicue (see Cisneros's story "Little Miracles, Kept Promises"). The expectation for Latinas is that they will become wives and mothers and hold the family together at any cost: "Those within the Latino community expect Latinas to be traditional, and to exist solely within the Latino family structure. A Latina must serve as a daughter, a wife, and a parent, and must place the needs of the family members above her own" (Rivera 502). The formidable culture of Latino patriarchy and machismo will be redefined as women struggle against dictatorships and/or emergent new societies like the United States during the sixties.

All authors included here have something to say about gender, about how men and women live in separate worlds, and about how they interact with each other. Ortiz Cofer's *cuentos* typically deal with Puerto Rican women and the hardships they face while also addressing the plight of young working Puerto Rican men, who are unemployed or transferred to the mainland in order to support their families. Indeed, her novel *The Line of the Sun* is about women both on the island and in New Jersey. Ortiz Cofer tries specifically to debunk the myth of the Latina woman as a "whore, domestic worker or criminal" ("Hers" 136). But, Ortiz Cofer, like Cisneros, also recognizes the difficulties the male Latino faces in terms of racial discrimination and pay inequities. Cisneros, in her story "Woman Hollering Creek" describes the hardships Cleófilas's husband and friends endure for the sake of job security. In *Bless Me, Ultima,* Anaya also addresses this issue when Antonio's father struggles in his job, building a highway on which he will never travel. Junot Díaz's story "Negocios" provides another example of the expectations placed on the Latino male, who is supposed to provide for his family at all costs.

When the daughters rebel, as they do in most of the Latina novels, they are tempted by the possibilities inherent in the ideas, customs, and traditions of their new world. In each case, how to adjust to, adopt, or reject these new ideas creates the struggle through which the characters change. One way to address the conflict between the old and the new is to rename the self or readdress old world traditions. Cisneros's characters provide a prime example of the renaming of the self and of the reinventing of myths and traditions. But, other authors also play with the concept of name and how it changes on the mainland. Not only are the naming of Latino communities important, but many authors create characters who play with the notion of renaming the self: Cisneros's character Esperanza and her story "Mericans," Quiñonez and the use of nicknames, Alvarez's multiple names for Yolanda, the protagonist in ¡*Yo*!

Along with the idea of reinventing the self is that of dominating the new language. Language plays an important role in the success of the individual. For example, Marisol's mother in *The Line of the Sun* fails to assimilate because she will not learn English. In Cisneros's story "No Speak English," the character does not leave her home because she cannot speak English. In Alvarez's *García Girls,* the mother continually mangles the English language much to the daughters' embarrassment, and the father never truly learns English, which always marks him as a foreigner. Without English, characters become literally trapped in their buildings, homes, or apartments. However, Spanish remains important in the creation of identity as well. In Quiñonez's novel, Spanish does not remain barricaded from change. Willie Bodega, a character in Ernesto Quiñonez's novel says that Spanglish, the mix of Spanish and English, can mean "a new race" (212). Anaya sees Spanish as the "soul of our culture" and, thus, it needs to be honored, taught, respected, and kept as a crucial element in the cultural expression of Chicanos and Latinos (Dash et al. 157). Cisneros sees it as a connection to her father and his Mexican past.

Religion plays a vital role in Latino culture and is addressed in all the fiction included here. Most Cubans, Puerto Ricans, Dominicans, and Mexican Americans are Catholic but harbor a syncretic spirituality from their African or indigenous past. *Santería, espiritismo,* Ultima's world, all are reflections of the African or indigenous roots of Latinos. The syncretism that emerged is largely a result of the Catholic aspect of the conquest. *Santería,* in fact, means "in the way of the saints," as practitioners of ancient African traditions would hide their pagan gods behind Catholic saints to fool the priests. In Quiñonez's novel, the Pentecostal Church is the primary religious center, but attention is also paid to *santería*. Yunior's mother, in "Fiesta, 1980," always blesses her children before they travel in the car, "We said, in turn, Bendición, Mami, and she poked us in our five cardinal spots while saying, Que Dios te bendiga" (27). She also tosses mints out the car window "an offering to Eshú" (28). Eshu, also known as Eleggua (Cuba), as seen in García's novel, is considered the owner of every road of life. His is the first place among the Orisha of the Yorubas of West Africa (Kafoed).

The religious elements of many novels present students with rich opportunities for analysis. For example, *In the Time of the Butterflies* portrays the traditional relationship between church and state that characterized the colonies of Spain for several centuries. The Mirabal daughters are devout Catholics, the oldest even aspiring to become a nun. But, slowly that devotion crumbles as the daughters become aware of the horrors of the Trujillo dictatorship and the role of the Catholic Church, which for most of the regime is a silent supporter of the evils of this dictator. At this revelation, the daughters question the role of the church as does the rest of Latin America in later years. The liberation theology that emerges will redefine the role of the Catholic Church in politics.

The eleven pieces of fiction included in this volume stand as creators of Latino culture, to use Greenblatt's words. Taken together, they exemplify the diversity among Latino communities. Readers will no longer be able to categorize Latinos in one group, as each piece of fiction offers a different tradition or approach to gender, religion, immigration, or exile. The themes presented in these novels and stories provide a compelling portrait of the differences among Latino cultures and communities across the nation. Further, this fiction not only allows students and readers a glimpse into different worlds, but also the opportunity to discover their own words as they compare what they read with how they live, form an identity, and search for roots. In this respect, this book hopes to celebrate not only Latino culture but also multitudes of cultures across the mainland.

NOTE

1. During the 1960s Mexican Americans appropriated what was a derogatory term and celebrated it. In the early days of Mexican immigration, the term "Mechicano" meant working-class Mexican immigrant. "Because the students, laborers, and political workers of the 1960s saw themselves as working class, they began to use the term as a badge of political affirmation and positive identity. Chicanos were Mexican Americans with their political and cultural consciousness raised" (Kanellos 8). "Nuyoricans" means Puerto Ricans born or raised in New York: "The ones who were bilingual, bicultural and identified with the metropolis began calling themselves Nuyoricans" (Kanellos 8). *Boricuas* is the Taíno name for Puerto Ricans, *Quisqueya*, the native name for Dominicans, *tejano*, the name of Mexicans before the United States annexed the Southwest.

OTHER SUGGESTED READINGS

Coerver, Don and Linda Hall, eds. *Tangled Destinies: Latin America and the United States.* Albuquerque: The University of New Mexico Press, 1999.

Gonzalez, Juan. *Harvest Empire: A History of Latinos in America.* New York: Viking, 2000.

Luis, William. *Dance between Two Cultures: Latino Caribbean Literature Written in the United States.* Nashville and London: Vanderbilt University Press, 1997.

Martinez, Oscar J. *Mexican-Origin People in the United States: A Topical History.* Tucson: The University of Arizona Press, 2001.

Morales, Carrión Arturo. *Puerto Rico: A Political and Cultural History.* New York: W. W. Norton & Co., 1983.

Moya Pons, Frank. *The Dominican Republic: A National History.* Princeton: Markus Wiener Publishers, 1998.

Novas, Himilce. *Everything You Need to Know about Latino History.* New York and London: Plume, 1994.

Pérez Jr., Louis A. *Cuba: Between Reform and Revolution.* New York and Oxford: Oxford University Press, 1995.

Rivera, Jenny. "Domestic Violence against Latinas by Latino Males." *The Latino Condition: A Critical Reader.* Ed. Richard Delgado and Jean Stefancic. New York and London: New York University Press, 1998. 501–507.

Rogozinski, Jan. *A Brief History of the Caribbean: From the Arawak and Carib to the Present.* New York and London: Plume, 2000.

Roorda, Eric. *The Dictator Next Door: The Good Neighbor Policy and the Trujillo Regime in the Dominican Republic, 1930–1945 (American Encounters/ Global Interactions).* Durham and London: Duke University Press, 1998.

"Crucible of Empire." War of 1898 Interactive Web Center. <http://pbs.org>

Chapter 1

The Fiction of Julia Alvarez: How the García Girls Lost Their Accents (1992) and In the Time of the Butterflies (1995)

J ulia Alvarez was born in New York in 1950. A year later, her parents
returned to the Dominican Republic, where she lived until the age of
ten. Alvarez's father was actively involved in the underground movement to overthrow the Dominican dictator of three decades, Rafael
Leonidas Trujillo. When her father's activities became increasingly suspicious, the family fled to New York again in 1960. The reasons for their
abrupt departure were concealed from Alvarez and her three sisters; her
mother simply told them they were leaving for the beach. Alvarez later
reflected on this deception in her essay "Our Papers": "I would wonder if
those papers [visas to leave the island] had set us free from everything we
loved" (*Something to Declare* 19). Alvarez had, in many respects, lost a
homeland. Although she would return years later, the Dominican Republic
that she had known and experienced as a child was unrecoverable.

Alvarez's love of the English language and writing began at an early age.
In the Dominican Republic, her mother encouraged her daughters to learn
English and provided them with an American education. In New York,
Alvarez remembers a sixth-grade English teacher who nurtured her love of
reading, writing, and language. Alvarez went on to study literature at
Connecticut College, and then at Syracuse University. After spending many

years as a part-time writing and English teacher throughout the country, she became a creative-writing professor at Middlebury College, where she continues to work today. This "Vermont writer from the Dominican Republic," as Alvarez describes herself, has written four novels, three books of poetry, and one book of essays. Her novels, *How the García Girls Lost Their Accents* (1992), *In the Time of the Butterflies* (1995), *¡Yo!* (1997), and *In the Name of Salomé* (2000), communicate two important themes in her work, a search for identity and an exploration of history. Alvarez has received widespread recognition as one of the most important and diverse Latina writers in the last few decades. Alvarez's work, as a whole, portrays the life of Latinos, in particular Dominicans, as they struggle to adapt to life in the United States, and gives voice to the history of the Dominican Republic.

Alvarez's fictional world mirrors her personal world. Like many of her characters, Alvarez embarked on a journey to discover her identity and that of her island. Her evolution as a writer has been permanently influenced by her conflicted and continued search for meaning within her bilingual and bicultural identity, and for the history of her island. Alvarez's themes come from her past as an exiled Dominican who arrived in New York in 1960, facing, as she says, "new-world pressures and an old-world style" (Heredia and Kevane 22). Alvarez found education and writing viable solutions for learning how to live as a person with two cultures. Now, after more than twenty-two years of writing and teaching, she has also defined her ultimate goal in writing: it is to immerse her readers within the world of the exiled communities in the United States and within the world of her island's culture. Fiction, she believes, is the vehicle that can transmit this culture to North American readers. The history of the Dominican Republic and its people, according to Alvarez, "can only finally be understood by fiction, only finally be redeemed by the imagination. A novel is not, after all, a historical document, but a way to travel through the human heart" (*In the Time of the Butterflies* 324).

This chapter focuses on Alvarez's two best-known and most popular novels, *How the García Girls Lost Their Accents* (referred to as *García Girls*) and *In the Time of the Butterflies* (referred to as *Butterflies*). Readers might also be interested in Alvarez's other two novels, *¡Yo!* and *In the Name of Salomé*, not only because they contain the themes that characterize her work but also because they reveal her evolution as a writer. Alvarez's third novel, *¡Yo!*, returns to the main protagonist of *García Girls*, Yolanda García, further exploring the making of a bilingual and bicultural identity. It is the portrait of an artist, but one with a twist: everybody except the artist herself narrates stories about Yolanda. Her family, friends, lovers, servants, and others tell contradictory and, oftentimes, unflattering tales about Yolanda. It is up to the reader to believe or not believe the multiple tales and to create his or her own portrait of Yolanda. *Salomé*, Alvarez's most recent novel, describes the life of Salomé Ureña, the national poet of the Dominican Republic in the nineteenth century, and the political upheaval in which she lived. In this latest book, Alvarez returns to the earlier years of the formation of the Dominican Republic and reveals how the poetry of Ureña inspired politicians and citizens alike to create a democratic and independent nation. In these parallel works one can trace Alvarez's evolution and her attempt to delve deeper into the issues concerning identity and history. Because of her devotion to these themes, we have today a complex record of the Dominican Republic, a record of both Dominicans/*dominicanos* on the island and the diaspora of the *dominican-yorks* (Dominicans from or living in New York), as the father of the García clan calls himself.

Julia Alvarez's first novel, *How the García Girls Lost Their Accents,* is a fictional autobiography that describes the García family's exile to New York in 1960 when they, like so many other Dominicans, fled the Trujillo regime. *García Girls* chronicles the experiences of the García de la Torre family, particularly the four daughters, as they adjust to life in New York. Alvarez vividly captures the difficulties the sisters face in adapting to an American lifestyle, especially as their arrival coincides with the advent of the turbulent sixties in the United States.

Narrated in reverse chronological order, from 1989 to 1956, the novel spans thirty-three years and follows this Dominican family through a series of connected stories. The stories center on Yolanda García and, to a lesser extent, her sisters—Carla, the oldest, Sandi, the second oldest, and Sofía, the youngest. The plot traces the lives of the "four girls," as the mother calls them, with alternating narrative viewpoints: first person, third person omniscient, and first person plural. The first person "I" narrative is reserved for instances that are meant to stand out. For example, in Part III of the novel, the one non-García member, the Haitian servant Chucha, is given a first-person narration. Similarly, the earliest childhood memories of each daughter are narrated in the first person "I." First person plural, in turn, depicts the four sisters in a "we" voice, which characterizes their collective struggle to accommodate themselves to two worlds. The multiple narrative voices testify to a range of experiences that are meant to expand our understanding of the bicultural and bilingual world. In employing this narrative structure, Alvarez embraces what many contemporary Latina writers have acknowledged; there is no one official Latino history or diaspora experience. All of the characters in the García family experience their exile in a different manner.

The title of Alvarez's first novel is symbolic and significant to the narration itself. Although the title specifically refers to the "loss" of a Spanish accent, it is symbolic of the larger cultural losses suffered by immigrants as they struggle to survive in the United States. The loss of a homeland, relatives, family, house, food, music, clothing—in essence, the loss of a way of life—can rarely, if ever, be reclaimed or replaced. This loss, however, is bittersweet because it is the price to be paid in order to escape political repression, incarceration, torture, death, or economic stagnation. Although the title does not speak of positive changes, readers will sense that there are gains for many of the characters: freedom from a repressive dictatorship; from restrictive gender roles; and from a patriarchal system in which women do not have access to social, economic, and political opportunities. In this sense, *How the García Girls Lost Their Accents* refers to the losses and gains suffered not only by the García family, but by all exile or immigrant families.

The fifteen interrelated chapters that narrate the history of the García family in reverse chronological order are divided into three parts, with five chapters each. These parts depict three important stages in the life of this exiled family: Part I, which opens the novel in the present, describes the outcomes or unresolved issues that are a product of living in a bilingual and bicultural atmosphere; Part II depicts various cultural encounters and challenges that the sisters and their parents face upon arriving in New York; and Part III provides the context, life in the Dominican Republic before the family is forced into exile. This section describes life on the island, the homeland, before everything changed. In addition, this last section sharply contrasts with the previous two parts because it takes place on the island. It serves as the key to unlocking the characters in the novel and helps the reader to better understand the whole novel. In this sense, the novel resembles something of a puzzle that the reader, upon finishing, will be inclined to return to in order to put the pieces together.

How the García Girls Lost Their Accents (1992)

PART I (1989–1972)

Part I of the book depicts the García family from 1989 to 1972. These five chapters, which cover the adult lives of the four daughters, reveal the struggles that the sisters endure in their desire to belong to the North American culture and yet remain loyal to the traditions of their parents and to their early Hispanic heritage. The first chapter, "Antojos" ("Cravings"), describes Yolanda's return to the Dominican Republic. This chapter reflects on one of the most important cultural elements of bicultural literature, the return to the homeland. "The Kiss," the following chapter, captures the gender clashes that emerge given the rules of the world from which they came and those of the world in which they now live. This chapter focuses on the particular traditions of the García family and exposes some of the difficulties the sisters faced while growing up in an increasingly liberal country with a "strict traditional father" (107).

In the third chapter, "The Four Girls," Alvarez offers the reader two diametrically opposed narratives about the daughters. In the first section of this chapter the mother describes superficial anecdotes about her daughters. The second section, however, narrates the "true stories" of the daughters as they gather in a bedroom to gossip. The reader can recognize the difference between the little nostalgic anecdotes that the mother cherishes from the past and the present condition of the daughters, who have become sexually liberated, one who has been mentally institutionalized, and who have had "many husbands, homes, jobs, wrong turns among them" (11).

Chapter four continues to defy the mother's romanticized version of her daughters' lives, as it narrates Yolanda's mental breakdown and divorce from her first husband. This chapter, entitled "Joe," is also an important chapter because it highlights the connection for Yolanda between language and identity. "The Rudy Elmenhurst Story," the closing chapter of Part I, depicts Yolanda's first year in college. In keeping with the theme found in the previous chapter, we again witness Yolanda's personal struggle with language and identity.

PART II (1970–1960)

If the first part of *How the García Girls Lost Their Accents* depicts the unresolved issues that form the identities of this exiled family, Part II, from 1970–1960, depicts cultural conflicts. Part II shows the evolution of the sisters as they experience homesickness and painful experiences such as racism. They emerge as four well-adjusted young women who have discovered power in their adopted country and feel disdain for the culture left behind. The first chapter, in particular, narrated in the first person plural "we," represents a temporary phase of complete devotion to and adoption of the new culture. The next four chapters, however, deal with the unease and pain of not belonging during their first months on the mainland.

"A Regular Revolution" opens with the four sisters showing off their American identities, having more than adjusted to the freedom they have attained on the mainland. In this chapter, the four sisters exhibit a strong sense of pride and excitement, and a certain revolutionary attitude about being Americans/*americanas*. The second chapter, "Daughter of Invention," focuses on both Laura García, the mother, and Yolanda. The title of the chapter again reflects the content of the chapter, as both Laura and Yolanda reinvent themselves in the United States. In the first half of this section Laura discovers that in the United States she can shed the constraints of her family name and do whatever she likes. The second section portrays Yolanda as the budding writer. The following two chapters, "Trespass" and "Snow," depict the first few years of the family's exile in the United States. "Trespass" deals with racism and the confrontation Carla, the oldest, faces in a hostile space. "Snow" reflects a positive experience as Yolanda is nurtured by her teachers in her early years. Both titles reflect what the characters feel, trespassing in a new country, and experiencing an element alien to the Caribbean, snow. Analyzed together, both of these chapters reveal how linguistic and cultural differences can create either painful or wonderful situations.

The last chapter of this section, "Floor Show," portrays the cultural encounters of the whole family in their first months in New York. Told from the point of view of Sandi, the second eldest daughter, the chapter realistically portrays the growing awareness of the family that they no longer hold the privileged position of an affluent Dominican family. Rather, they have entered a new category of immigrants. With typical childlike and incisive observations, Sandi notices the awkward dynamic between the two cultures, the paternal American culture and the desperate Dominican culture. The proud García de la Torre family patriarch, Carlos, has been stripped of his machismo, job, and power; he now finds himself at the beck and call of his American friends.

PART III (1960–1956)

Part III of the novel depicts the traditions and habits of the García de la Torre clan in their homeland, the Dominican Republic. The stories take place from 1960 to 1956, the year the García family escapes to New York. It provides the context for our understanding of the family. It also illustrates several elements of the family dynamic: there are servants, nannies, secluded grounds, and access to an elite American education, as the mother attempts to raise the girls "American style" (203). Despite these economic luxuries, it is also a family (and nation) living in daily terror because of the Trujillo regime. Alvarez deftly contrasts the two levels that characterize life on the compound—the childish games, events, and crises that make up the children's world versus the terror and fear of the adult world. The adults live with the knowledge that they can be discovered and taken away by Trujillo's henchmen, the SIM (Military Intelligence Services), or the *cálies* (secret police), as they are known on the island.

The first chapter in Part III, "The Blood of the Conquistadores," is of particular cultural value. It is divided into two sections. The first section portrays one of the most feared and dreaded events for Dominican families, a visit by the SIM, Trujillo's secret police, which results in the family's exile to New York. The second section contains a eulogy, of sorts, to the island. It is narrated by two characters—the youngest daughter Sofía, nicknamed Fifi, "the one who doesn't remember anything from that last day on the Island because I'm the youngest"; and Chucha, the Haitian servant, who also experienced exile and was never able to return to her homeland.

The remaining chapters in Part III contain the rest of the first-person narrations of the daughters, Yolanda, Sandi, and Carla. Each sister narrates one childhood memory that is meant to serve as a key to the interpretation of her contemporary identity as an adult. "The Drum," the last chapter of the novel, is narrated by Yolanda. The last paragraph of this chapter serves as a kind of epilogue, as it provides a context for Yolanda's passion for the written word and her desire to become a writer. Recalling how she stole a helpless kitten from a mother cat, Yolanda describes how the event created a recurring nightmare meant to be understood in symbolic terms: "At that hour and in that loneliness, I hear her [the mother cat], a black furred thing lurking in the corners of my life, her magenta mouth opening, wailing over some violation that lies at the center of my art" (290). Just as Yolanda tore the kitten away from the mother, she has been torn away from her motherland. It is this experience, forever rendered in terms of loss (just as the kitten was forever lost to its mother), that lies at the center of her identity and that will lie at the center of her fictional work. The violation is the exile, the act of being torn from the homeland, never able to return.

CULTURAL ELEMENTS

The cultural story in *How the García Girls Lost Their Accents* begins with the García family's departure from the Dominican Republic in 1956 and ends with Yolanda's return to the homeland in 1989. Between these two points in time, the reader will discover a wealth of clashing cultural elements that emerge from the traditions left behind and the new culture found on the mainland. At the center of the cultural narrative is the search for a balanced ethnic identity, manifested especially through Yolanda, within the new and old cultural traditions. The characters live out and experience their contradictions in private and public ways. The daughters attempt to reconcile their desire to become "Americanized," liberated women with modern dreams of careers and success with their desire to remain good Catholic daughters, *hijas buenas* (good daughters), tied by tradition to their father and to their island. The parents struggle as well with this conflict between old and new cultural traditions. Although both parents want their daughters to belong—to become "Americanized" by "ironing" out their accents, for example—they only want this Americanization to go so far. They believe that the end goal for their daughters should be marriage to a respectable Dominican man from the island. The parents, like the daughters, suffer the dramatic impact of exile. Upon arrival in the United States, Carlos García, the patriarch of the family, is stripped of his identity. During their early months in New York, he is like any other immigrant, jobless, helpless, and almost speechless, as he does not speak the language fluently. Laura García, on the other hand, enjoys the freedom from her family compound and the anonymity that life as a Latina immigrant grants her. Nevertheless, the main focus of the novel rests on the problems and anxieties that the daughters experience. These problems and anxieties are particular to immigrant daughters of traditional Hispanic households who are attempting to partic-ipate in a new culture while remaining faithful to their origins.

In addition to the richness of cultural details found in the three parts of the novel, we have the story of Yolanda García and her creation of an eth-nic identity. Her journey and struggle, portrayed in reverse chronological order, is that of a writer who has finally found a voice and an identity through the written word. From her earliest memories—through her year in high school, her first year in college, her first marriage, divorce, break-down, and finally her return to the island—her struggles toward a more balanced identity, toward a mediation of two cultures, is the most vividly illustrated in the novel. Of the fifteen chapters in the novel, seven are devoted solely to Yolanda, and two others prominently include her. Yolanda opens and closes the novel and encompasses the most important themes of immigrant literature—return to homeland, struggles with language, strug-gle with gender roles, and a desire to communicate experience.

The first chapter opens with Yolanda's return to the homeland. Although it is 1989, life on the family compound still follows the "mighty wave of tra-dition" (9) as Yolanda describes it. The women still maintain the traditional role of housewife, and the men still enjoy their patriarchal status that includes such expected privileges as the "Whore Hour," a predinner hour with a mistress. Despite her observation that life on the island has not evolved as she has, Yolanda attempts to fit in, to belong to this home that she left behind as a young girl.

At the age of thirty-nine, Yolanda believes that a return home will provide the answers to the conflicts that the reader has witnessed in reverse chrono-logical order. "Antojos," the only Spanish chapter title in the novel, can be translated as "a craving for something you have to eat," or a person "taken over by *un santo* [a saint] who wants something." It is an appropriate title in that it represents Yolanda's craving both for the guavas that she remem-bers from her childhood—a small, pale yellow tropical fruit with a pink rich-tasting flesh—but also, and more importantly, a craving for a sense of self or a return to a long-lost self. Although Yolanda will be able to eat guavas again, the pleasure is marred by the realization that she will not be able to return to her homeland.

In her search for guavas, Yolanda ventures out to the center of the island; she is already breaking with the traditions that rule the island since women do not travel alone. When Yolanda's car breaks down and two *campesinos* (farmers) come to help her, she is unable to communicate with the men and is estranged from the situation. She initially fears the *campesinos* not only because they are men and she is a woman, but also because her cousins have warned her of "incidents." Yolanda, out of fear, speaks to them in English. When they conclude that she is an *americana,* she is relieved because she feels protected by that identity. As she returns to the family compound, the reader can feel her sense of failure and her quiet recognition that the

Dominican Republic is no longer her home. This chapter illustrates an important issue in ethnic literature—the difficulty in returning to the homeland. Yolanda is no longer fluent in Spanish, and she no longer lives by the social rules of the island. At thirty-nine, she is a divorced woman with no children, no job, and no secure future. She is incapable of identifying herself completely as a *dominicana* and rests heavily on her *norteamericana* identity. Alvarez emphasizes that though her character may return, she will never again be "all island."

Alvarez depicts Yolanda's deep yearning and the difficulties faced by an immigrant returning home. Yolanda's linguistic obstacle, the Americanization of her identity, and the cultural inheritance of another nation, all contribute to her realization that the island remains lost to her in the way she had remembered it. In this respect, this chapter raises the fundamental questions that pertain to all exile literature: Where does Yolanda belong now that she has lived on the mainland more years than she has on the island? To which culture does she relate? Where is home? What is her language, English or Spanish? As someone who was forced to leave the homeland, not given any choice, questions like these will haunt Yolanda for the rest of her life.

Alvarez's novel also raises fundamental questions that concern all individuals: What is the importance of a homeland? Of belonging? What is lost when you leave one culture and enter another? Is it the homeland, food, music, dress, or a sense of self? What would it be like never to be able to return home, to learn another language, to lose childhood family and friends? For the characters in *How the García Girls Lost Their Accents*, as for Alvarez herself, the answer to these questions lies in a balance of the losses and gains of cultural elements. Alvarez consciously demonstrates, especially in the case of Yolanda, that some losses, like the homeland, will never be fully reclaimed. Years of living alienated from the homeland create a permanent awareness of difference. Loss, however, is accompanied by gains. The loss of a dress code, that of the "hair-and-nail cousins" that identifies the individual as a certain type of Dominican, is replaced by what Yolanda learns is a missionary look—sandals, wild hair, long loose skirt, "like one of those Peace Corps girls who have let themselves go" (4). The loss of the maternal language is complemented by the acquisition of another, English. The loss of the extended and insular family, like that of the García family on the compound, is replaced by a freedom to move, to make a home elsewhere among different communities.

In the Time of the Butterflies (1995)

In the Time of the Butterflies is based on the true story of the four Mirabal sisters from the Dominican Republic, and on their struggle against the dictatorship of Rafael Leonidas Trujillo, who ruled from 1930–1961. The Mirabal sisters, born in the mid-twenties and thirties on the island, have become international heroes. Many Latin American countries honor the date of their murder, November 25, as the International Day Against Violence Towards Women. Alvarez initially intended to write a biography about the sisters' lives. However, as she reports in her essay "Chasing the Butterflies," her search for the real story about the sisters revealed as many truths as fictions. In addition, everyone claimed to have *the* story about *las muchachas* (the girls), as they are affectionately called on the island. Alvarez decided that the best way to convey the history of these courageous sisters was through a novel (*Something to Declare* 202).

Although *Butterflies*, an historical novel, reflects a major departure for Alvarez in terms of subject matter, it provides an enriching complement to her more popular novel, *García Girls*. It would be worthwhile to read both of these novels, as they not only reveal Alvarez's profound evolution as a writer, but also expand the knowledge readers will gain about the Dominican Republic. Identity issues are prevalent in both books. In *Butterflies*, each sister undergoes a transformation, from innocent adolescent to revolutionary woman, with the Trujillo dictatorship serving as the catalyst for this change. For the García family, the dictatorship means exile; for the Mirabal sisters, the dictatorship means death. Similarities exist between the two novels. Both novels describe the lives of four sisters from the Dominican Republic and the effects of dictatorship on a family. The books share a similar narrative structure: both novels are divided into three parts, with chapters alternating between the sisters. However, in *García Girls*, Yolanda was given the most chapters, and in *Butterflies* each part is evenly split, with each sister given three chapters. In this respect, Alvarez again employs several different viewpoints. Each novel begins in the present and returns to the past. *García Girls* actually travels in reverse chronological order (1989–1956), whereas *Butterflies* begins in the present, 1994, continues by narrating events from 1948 to 1960, and then jumps back to the present to end the novel. Both novels portray a period of innocence and peace before the dramatic change that causes the action of the novel, exile in *García Girls* and dictatorship in *Butterflies*. These traumatic political events forever disrupt family life for the characters of these novels. Also, both novels have a narrator who unifies and links the diverse voices, Yolanda García in *García Girls* and Dedé Mirabal in *Butterflies*.

If identity were the framework through which we studied culture in *García Girls*, history, specifically Trujillo's thirty-one year reign, would be the framework in *Butterflies*. *In the Time of the Butterflies* reveals culture through the political dynamic of a dictatorship. It demonstrates how a dictatorship changes a community, a culture, and its people to almost unrecognizable dimensions. How does a dictatorship affect culture and cultural institutions such as religion or family? What happens to a culture when its people are not allowed freedom of expression, and when human rights are abused? What happens when a culture is warped to serve the sole purpose of deifying a dictator? Trujillo designated himself "El Jefe," "El Benefactor," and "El Generalísimo." His picture hung in every household, and his slogan was "Dios y Trujillo" (God and Trujillo) Trujillo created a cult of megalomania that his citizens had to mimic. Alvarez, in her essay about life under Trujillo, says, "Dominicans had learned the habit of repression, censorship, terror. Those habits would not disappear with a few bullets and a national liberation proclamation" (*Something to Declare* 107). Indeed, the opening scene of the novel, though taking place more than thirty years after Trujillo's assassination, reflects the difficulty in forgetting hard-learned habits from a dictatorship. Dedé, the only surviving sister of the Mirabal sisters, awaits a woman who wants to interview her. When the woman finally arrives, she slams her door shut, making Dedé jump, reminding her of the SIM's (Trujillo's ubiquitous Military Intelligence Service) unexpected visits.

The title of the book, *In the Time of the Butterflies*, contains a play on words. Butterflies, *las mariposas*, is the code name for the three sisters in the underground movement. The thirty-one years of Trujillo's dictatorship became known as "La era de Trujillo" ("The Time/Era of Trujillo"). Alvarez consciously alludes to this historical period that spanned three decades but cleverly inserts the code name for the revolutionary sisters, *las mariposas*, butterflies, instead of Trujillo. In this way she emphasizes an alternative history of the era, one silenced by the dictator. Alvarez incorporates the voices of the marginalized groups that fought to overthrow the dictatorship and makes them part of official history. Finally, on a symbolic level, butterflies refer to the transformation, the metamorphosis of the sisters. Like butterflies, the sisters undergo three stages to reach the completion of their transformation from young, innocent girls to revolutionary women.

There are three parts to this novel. Each part contains four chapters, one for each Mirabal sister. Part I is the shortest of the novel, whereas Parts II and III are more than double the size. Each part opens with Dedé, whose narration takes place in the third person, unlike the rest of the sisters. In turn, each of Dedé's chapters is divided into two parts, the first taking place in the present, 1994, and the second taking place in the past, beginning in 1943. For example, in Chapter 1 of Part I, the novel begins in the present, 1994, with Dedé meeting the *gringa dominicana* who will be interviewing her and then, prompted by a question from the "interview woman" (6), it moves back in time to 1943. Employing an interview as the framework for the novel serves two important functions: it marks the temporal framework for the action of the novel, a couple of hours, and it serves as a catharsis and final transformation for the surviving sister, Dedé. The time frame of the novel transpires from three o'clock in the afternoon until the end of evening. However, each question asked by the interviewer sends the reader and Dedé back in time from 1938 to 1960, tracing the evolution of the

Mirabal sisters from innocence to active involvement in the revolutionary underground. As in Alvarez's first novel, narrative voice switches from first person to third person, given the character. The three murdered sisters narrate in first person, María Theresa in diary form, whereas Dedé is mostly in third person, until the epilogue. Students should pay careful attention to these switches, as they are very revealing about the characters. For instance, why is it that the voices of the murdered sisters are in first person if these are memories recounted by Dedé for the interviewer? The importance of focusing on these narrative details is to demonstrate how Alvarez's technique is evolving and creating a more complex narration.

PART I: 1994, 1938 AND 1941–1946

Part I of *Butterflies* describes the meeting between Dedé Mirabal, the second oldest and only surviving sister, and the *gringa dominicana* (who remains nameless, but who might be Alvarez's alter ego), who has come to the Dominican Republic to interview Dedé about her sisters. Prompted by the questions of the interviewer, the novel begins with Dedé's recollections of a time of innocence prior to the complications with the Trujillo regime. This first part of the novel, with each chapter narrated by one of the sisters in the first person, reveals the seeds of doubt experienced by each of the sisters toward their beloved president. These seeds will grow in each sister, and Minerva, Patria, and María Teresa, will evolve radically in terms of their attitude toward Trujillo. Each sister is exposed to a particular story or event about Trujillo that will begin the process of her transformation from an innocent young girl to an active revolutionary and agent of change. Minerva's change is instigated by her classmate, Sinita Perozo, whose brothers and uncles are killed by Trujillo; Mate's (María Teresa's nickname) and Patria's doubts are the result of Minerva's activities. Each sister's sense of security and trust in Trujillo is shattered by the end of Part I. In addition, these first chapters attest to the culture of Trujillo, the many celebrations, holidays, and customs, and the politics of his regime. We learn of the Catholic Church's early support of the dictator, the disappearance of many Dominicans, the revision of history books, the fear and suspicion he created in families, and the psychological power he wielded over an entire nation.

PART II: 1994, 1948–1959

Part II begins with a question posed by the interviewer: "When did all the problems start?" (65). According to Dedé, as with Mate and Patria, the troubles began with Minerva. At the same time, those troubles led to an awareness that, as Dedé now realizes, they "were really living in a police state" (75).

Alvarez aptly describes the bureaucracy that accompanied the Trujillo regime, the dos and don'ts that families had to follow in order to survive. These chapters reveal the sacrifice that accompanied being involved in any subversive activities. Because of Minerva's involvement, the Mirabal sisters' father is imprisoned. Upon his release, the family realizes that Enrique Mirabal's spirit has been broken, and shortly afterward he dies. By the end of Part II, we have witnessed a complete transformation of all of the sisters, except Dedé.

PART III: JANUARY 1960 TO NOVEMBER 25, 1960

Part III describes the final struggle, the imprisonment, and the assassination of Minerva, Patria, and Mate. It contains many historical references to the final year of Trujillo's regime, during which he began an increasingly hostile and paranoid campaign against any individual who was slightly suspicious. In addition, it describes the increasingly strained relations between Trujillo and the Catholic Church. As priests across the country began to denounce Trujillo, the dictator began a campaign against the church, accusing it of "stirring up trouble" (218). In addition, it describes a visit by American journalists and the OAS (Organization of American States), who were attempting to assess the Trujillo situation. The sisters' imprisonment speaks to the complex network that characterized prison life for political prisoners, or those who "can be snuffed out just like that" (238). It portrays the difficulty the prisoners faced: trying to keep sane, trying to maintain a sense of self, and trying not to give in to fear.

The epilogue is narrated by Dedé and, for the first time, in first person. We learn the details of the Mirabal sisters' death through the testimony of the many informants who visited Dedé after what was described as their "car accident," in the official report. Because it was evident to all that Trujillo had had them assassinated, strangers traveled to the Mirabal home to give Dedé the last details of her sisters' lives. They tell the story as they witnessed it, creating an unofficial oral account of what happened to the sisters. Each story contributes to the portrait of their last hours—that of the soldier, the attendant, the truck driver, and the man who walked for miles from the mountains just to tell Dedé the exact hour of the accident. "Each visitor would break my heart all over again, but I would sit on this very rocker and listen for as long as they had something to say. It was the least I could do, being the one saved" (301).

Dedé becomes the oracle for the whole Trujillo Era. As her husband tells her upon the sisters' death, now she will suffer her own martyrdom, being "the one left behind to tell the story of the other three" (203). Slowly, her recovery begins, as does that of the Dominican people. But it is a long journey, as the aftermath of the Trujillo dictatorship leads to civil wars, coups d'etat, and another U.S. Marine invasion in 1965. As Dedé says of her country, "We had them [civil wars] regularly, as if to prove we could kill each other even without a dictator to tell us to" (304). Dedé summarizes the rest of the lives of the husbands and children of her sisters, bringing us back to the present. Her one final rhetorical question, however, bitterly speaks to the secret fear she carries within her. At a reception honoring her sisters, she observes the new society emerging years after the dictatorship: "Boy-businessmen with computerized watches and walkie-talkies in their wives' purses to summon the chauffeur from the car; their glamorous young wives with degrees they do not need; the scent of perfume; the tinkle of keys to the things they own," and she wonders, "Was it for this, the sacrifice of the butterflies?" (318).

CULTURAL ELEMENTS

In the Time of the Butterflies portrays the emergence of a temporary culture of accommodation whose main goal became survival. It is a culture born from the repressive thirty-one year dictatorship. Because of the collision between the Trujillo regime and the Mirabal family, it is impossible to separate the intimate family history of the characters from the events that defined Trujillo's regime. During the regime, individuals were trained to obey out of fear: fear of the spies controlled speech, travel, and interaction with people; fear of censors controlled books, newspapers, and literary and artistic expression; fear of the SIM controlled uprisings. Few cultural institutions remained unaffected by the Trujillo regime; family, religion, dissemination of information, music, and even food were altered during these decades. Most families, whether or not they supported the regime, became cautious in words and deeds, resigned to the dictatorship, and determined to save their lives. Because of the length of the dictatorship, many generations of children grew up within the confines of the restrictive laws of Trujillo and, thus, maintained the status quo and rarely questioned their government. For his part, Trujillo, in order to retain complete power over supporters and opponents, did not reward loyalty. Because he maintained his power by requiring everyone to live under the threat of random violence, everyone had to be careful. Many times, his trujillista supporters, members of his Cabinet, ministers, and others were humiliated and thrown out of his inner circle for reasons they could not identify. At the same time, Trujillo randomly attacked families who had any connection, no matter how remote, to underground movements. Although the Mirabals were a rich, well-respected landowning agricultural family from the Cibao region, the sisters were directly involved in the J14 (abbreviated form of 14th June Movement). What happens to them is symbolic of the fate of all Dominican families. When we first meet the Mirabal family, they are already trained in the habits of caution and obedience, which were adopted for safety reasons. However, because of Minerva's growing awareness of oppression by the regime, the family members are transformed from silent witnesses to active revolutionaries, whether they want to be or not.

Trujillo, who rose to power with the support of the U.S. Marine Corps during its occupation of the island (Roorda 21–22), enforced severe measures immediately upon declaring himself the winner of fraudulent elections on August 16, 1930. In this way he was able to consolidate power while his country and his people grew more feeble. Not only did he appropriate "more than half of the industries in the Dominican Republic" (Zakrzewski Brown 31), creating a monopoly that devastated families, but he efficiently eliminated all political opponents and practiced censorship of periodicals and newspapers. He suppressed human rights, freedom of speech, and opposing political parties; he restricted physical mobility; and he stripped family industries and lands. Trujillo publicly flaunted his power through humiliation, torture, or death. Sometimes he displayed "carcasses with signs attached" (Zakrzewski Brown 31) in the streets to remind people of what might happen to them. If one member of a family was involved in any movement to overthrow him, he would go after the wife, children, siblings, or parents, as is portrayed in *Butterflies*. In agricultural regions like Cibao, Trujillo confiscated land, the patrimony of many families, if they were in any way involved in the underground. Thus, Pedro, Patria's husband, is incarcerated for allowing members of the underground to meet on his farm, even though he is not directly involved. Johnny Abbes, Trujillo's right-hand man, who appears in Alvarez's novel, was responsible for tortures of the most unimaginable kind, meted out to subversives or even those suspected of subversion. La Cuarenta, which also appears in the novel, was a notorious torture cell that haunted the dreams of many Dominican people.

Perhaps one of the more insidious changes accomplished by Trujillo was his ability to plant a little piece of himself in every Dominican citizen: "Dictatorships are pantheistic [spirit is identifiable in the natural world]," a character in Alvarez's novel explains, "The dictator manages to plant a little piece of himself in every one of us" (311). Alvarez creates this tone from the beginning of the novel when a small yet critical remark about Trujillo sends the entire family rushing inside. Dedé's first memory in the novel ends with the silence that falls on the otherwise happy group when her father mentions Trujillo in a less than complimentary way. When Minerva states that she wants to go to law school, her father's response prompts immediate silence, and the family imagines him as the subject of a report at SIM headquarters: "Suddenly, the dark fills with spies who are paid to hear things and report them down at Security. *Don Enrique claims Trujillo needs help in running this country. Don Enrique says it's about time women took over the government.* Words repeated, distorted, words recreated by those who might bear them a grudge, words stitched to words until they are the winding sheets the family will be buried in when their bodies are found dumped in a ditch, their tongues cut off for speaking too much" (10). Fear, which every individual carried within, created an auto-censure that operated constantly.

Families like the Mirabals, who were not supporters of the regime, nevertheless participated in the culture of unwavering adulation. Trujillo's portrait hung in their home, as in all Dominican homes. The Mirabal daughters did not initially question his portrait or the government under which they lived. *Viva Trujillo* (Long Live Trujillo) and *Trujillo es la Ley* (Trujillo is the Law) were common slogans spoken to express one's allegiance to the dictator. School history lessons taught of his providential ascension to power. His megalomania and delusions of grandeur manifested themselves through the many names he assigned himself—El Jefe, El Benefactor, El Generalísimo. In 1936, he renamed Santo Domingo, the capital of the island, Ciudad Trujillo. Parades, festivities, and holidays were created in his name, and lists were kept of people who were absent. These absences were later scrutinized, and the repercussions of an absence could be disastrous. The Mirabal family fails to bid Trujillo farewell at the Trujillo Discovery Day Dance (Part II, Chapter 2) and are terrified the next day. However, individuals who did not support the regime, yet who were afraid of joining the underground, engaged in small rebellious acts meant to exercise their limited freedom. For example, in one scene Alvarez describes the man who named his thirteen sons Pablo Antonio Almonte in order to outwit the regime: "Whichever son is caught can swear he isn't the brother they want!" (107). The allegorical play that Minerva and her high-school friends perform for Trujillo in one of the many celebrations for him is laden with secret criticism. These conditions characterized the nation during the Trujillo years and changed the morale of the country.

Social institutions underwent radical changes as well. In the novel, we witness the revolution within the Catholic Church. Patria abandons her traditional Catholic religious beliefs and embraces a revolutionary Catholicism, the main goal of which is to bring down the dictator. Traditional Catholic rituals are transformed when archbishops, priests, and nuns protest the dictatorship. The church, or parts of the Catholic Church's culture, changed in response to the atrocities committed by the regime. The culture of the church, one that propagated a certain resignation and nonviolence, became involved in active resistance against the regime. Sermons no longer ended in Amen but "Amen to the revolution." The new name of Patria's Church group, for example, was "Acción Clero-Cultural" (Action Cultural-Clergy). Its mission was to politically organize those Catholics who were willing to assume a nontraditional role as revolutionary agents of change. The nature of some sections of the church changed in order to mobilize a national underground.

The daughters in *Butterflies*, as the daughters in *García Girls*, experience shifts in family roles. The traditional patriarchal Mirabal family experiences a change in gender roles because of Trujillo. Enrique Mirabal is the passive leader of the household, whose spirit is broken by the regime; the daughters become active revolutionaries, whose spirits rise in their attempt to overthrow the dictator. In addition, children are no longer protected from politics but are seen as the future of the island. We witness Mate as she makes bombs and Patria's sixteen-year-old son as he counts ammunition in the name of the revolution.

Finally, the novel reveals the development of an underground culture that stands in direct contrast to the Trujillo culture. The core of the underground was made up of "cells" that were linked across the island. Each cell contained up to three members, who remained anonymous to all other members of the underground movement. When tortured, each revolutionary could only name two other individuals involved in the movement. Prison life for political prisoners remained linked to the cause. In the third and final part of the novel, Mate describes the place of confinement in which she and sixteen other women live for almost six months: metal bunks, a bucket, a tiny sink, and a tiny window, which the women take turns looking out of for ten minutes each day. A support system develops within the prison room in an attempt to assuage the inevitable breakdowns that all of the prisoners experience, some never recovering. The women give all of the guards code names, a game "that lets you know instantly what to expect from them. Bloody Juan, Little Razor, Good Hair" (231). Minerva, who becomes the leader of the group, trains the women to follow a schedule in order to maintain sanity and a semblance of an orderly life. Tricks to survive prison life include a little school, going to the movies in one's head, and cleaning the room in order to keep a high morale.

A new vocabulary was established in order to bypass the regime. Code names became a part of the common language between family, friends, and rebels, from *el chivo* (goat; the nickname for Trujillo) to tennis shoes (a code named used in *García Girls* for political emergency). In retaliation, Trujillo maintained the SIM, which also created a subculture of sorts. Although not captured in detail in *Butterflies*, the reader will recall the two country bumpkins in *García Girls*, who give voice to the nature of the SIM. Many poor *campesinos* (farmers) joined the SIM as a way out of poverty, not necessarily as Trujillo supporters. Once you joined the SIM, however, Trujillo enjoyed testing your loyalty. Families, religion, music (Trujillo's merengues), literature, and history books, were shattered, rewritten, altered, and forever changed. The regime successfully quelled its people. As the character Lío rhetorically asks: "This regime is seductive. How else would a whole nation fall prey to this little man?" (96).

A dictatorship, and the culture that emerges as a consequence, is a completely unfamiliar phenomenon to many North American readers. Alvarez's novel presents both those defeated by the Trujillo machine and those who attempted to defy it. There are characters in this novel, like the Mirabal sisters' father, who are eventually broken by the regime, and those whose spirits survive even after the regime has taken their lives.

FURTHER SUGGESTED READINGS

Works by Julia Alvarez

Alvarez, Julia. *Before We Were Free.* New York: Knopf, 2002.

———. *A Cafecito Story.* White River Junction: Chelsea Green Publishing Company, 2001.

———. *How Tía Lola Came to Stay.* New York: Knopf Book for Young Readers, 2001.

———. *In the Name of Salomé.* Chapel Hill: Algonquin Books, 2000.

———. *The Secret Footprints.* New York: Knopf Book for Young Readers, 2000.

———. *Something to Declare.* Chapel Hill: Algonquin Books, 1998.

———. *¡Yo!* Chapel Hill: Algonquin Books, 1997.

———. *The Other Side/El Otro Lado.* New York: Dutton, 1995.

———. *In the Time of the Butterflies.* Chapel Hill: Algonquin Books, 1994.

———. *How the García Girls Lost Their Accents.* Chapel Hill: Algonquin Books, 1991.

———. *Homecoming: New and Collected Poems.* New York: Grove Press, 1984.

———. *The Housekeeping Book.* Burlington: C.E.S. MacDonald, 1984.

Other Suggested Fiction

Cruz, Angie. *Soledad: A Novel.* New York: Scribner, 2002.

Díaz, Junot. *Drown.* New York: Riverhead Books, 1996.

Perez, Loida Maritza. *Geographies of Home.* New York: Penguin, 2000.

Rosaria, Nelly. *Song of the Water Saints.* New York: Vintage, 2003.

Chapter 2
The Fiction of Rudolfo Anaya: Bless Me, Ultima *(1972)*

Rudolfo Anaya was born in 1937 in Guadalupe County, New Mexico. He was one of seven children who were raised as Catholics and who spoke Spanish in their home in the small eastern village of Santa Rosa. When he was fifteen, Anaya's family moved to Albuquerque, where he graduated from high school in 1956. He received his B.A. in English from the University of New Mexico, and a master's in guidance and counseling in 1972, also from the University of New Mexico. Despite his education, Anaya states emphatically that he is a self-taught writer, never having taken a writing course. He attributes his passion for writing to the "old and wise *viejitos* [elders]" ("In Commemoration" 10), who taught him the magic of words and stories: "Now the words lie captured in ink, but the magic is still there, the power inherent in each volume. Now with book in hand we can participate in the wisdom of mankind" ("In Commemoration" 10). Enthralled by the words of the oral stories that were passed down to him, Anaya became passionate about learning to read the written word. His parents encouraged him to learn English, and Anaya found magic, too, in the English language: "I, who was used to reading my *oraciones en español* (sentences in Spanish) while I sat in the kitchen and answered the litany to the slap of my mother's tortillas, I now stumbled from sound to word to groups of words" and to the world of reading ("In Commemoration" 10). From this moment on Anaya would spend most of his time in the town library, a single room above the town's fire department, where he discovered infinite worlds to explore and where he also found "shelter and retreat" ("In Commemoration" 12).

It took Anaya seven years to write *Bless Me, Ultima,* which was originally published in 1972 by Quinto Sol Publications. Although Anaya is a prolific writer, *Bless Me, Ultima,* which won the Second Annual Premio Quinto Sol award, has remained his most respected and well-known novel. Today it is considered a classic of Chicano literature. *Bless Me, Ultima* became the first in what Anaya considers a trilogy of the trials and tribulations of adolescence in New Mexico. The second two novels, *Heart of Aztlán* (1976) and *Tortuga* (1979), follow the adolescent experiences of the Chávez boys, Jason and Benjie, in the urban barrio of Las Barelas in Albuquerque. *Tortuga* enforces the idea of the return to one's faith as an answer to modern-day trials. All of Anaya's novels contain autobiographical elements. For example, *Tortuga* stems from Anaya's hospitalization for a spinal injury as a child. In the novel, a young boy is burdened with a body cast. After Anaya's trilogy of the seventies, he wrote four novels in the nineties that also contribute to "his own unique view of *la Nueva México,* his vast historical romance rendered in a variety of narrative forms" (Calderón "Chicano Narrative" 111). In 1992, Anaya published *Albuquerque,* which was followed by his last three novels, *Zia Summer* (1995), *Rio Grande Fall* (1996) and *Shaman Winter* (1999), all murder mysteries solved by the detective Sonny Baca. In addition to his novels, Anaya has published collections of short stories, essays, and young adult fiction. Anaya, at one time, taught in the English department at the University of New Mexico, Albuquerque; he is now a full-time writer. Of writing, he says, "I have toyed with the idea that the writer is a shaman of sorts, who can affect the community to bring about a healing with story. This has always been a function of story. The fact that I write so much about *brujos* and *brujas,* who are shamans of our community, links me to that tradition" (Dash et al. 159).

Although Anaya shied away from the initial Chicano claims that novels had to be political, he has written political essays and has voiced his political opinions about Chicanos and their place in the United States. To understand his political beliefs, the reader might turn to Anaya's essay, "Aztlán: A Homeland without Boundaries" (Anaya and Lomelí, *Aztlán*). This essay emphasizes the long history of Chicanos on the mainland, specifically that of the mythical homeland of Aztlán, the land of the Aztecs in central Mexico. Chicanos in the sixties reclaimed Aztlán, the lost homeland, as a political move meant to emphasize the ancient history of Mexicans, thus granting them dignity in the face of Anglo colonization.

However, *Bless Me, Ultima* stands outside the political "Anglo-Chicano dialectic struggle" (Dash et al. 155), a struggle depicted in many of the other novels in this volume. The coming-of-age journey of the young Antonio Márez y Luna, the protagonist of the novel, does not encompass the conflict of finding one's place in mainstream America as an outsider or as a bilingual individual. When asked if *Bless Me, Ultima* is a political novel, Anaya responded, "Every novel is about self-identity. But if you say political it seems to me that [by that definition] you've got to show the struggle between our community and the mainstream Anglo-American community, that's the tension and that's what describes Chicano" (Dash et al. 156). *Bless Me, Ultima,* according to Anaya, does not fall into this category, as Antonio's struggle has little to do with the mainstream Anglo-American community. Nevertheless, the novel dispenses with the image of the "lazy" Mexican by creating complex individuals who work hard and have a complex history. When asked about his own political identity and consciousness, Anaya rattles off a series of labels meant to be inclusive, reflecting the complexity of the modern Chicano: "I'm Chicano, I'm American, I'm male, I'm *Nuevo Mexicano,* I'm southwesterner, I'm westerner" (Dash et al. 156).

Bless Me, Ultima is an autobiographical novel that explores the spiritual and personal journey of Antonio Márez y Luna, who is almost seven when the novel begins. The novel takes place in Guadalupe County, between Las Pasturas and El Puerto, the place where Anaya grew up. Antonio's parental heritage is like that of Anaya: Antonio's mother is from an El Puerto farming family, whereas his father is from a *vaquero* (cowboy) family whose location is the *llano* (plains) of Las Pasturas. Each location represents a long history of different lifestyles and traditions. In addition, the character Ultima is based on Anaya's grandmother, who was called *La Grande.* His grandmother, like Ultima, was a *curandera,* a folk healer with the knowledge and recognition of the power of herbs from *la tierra* (the earth), to heal both mental and physical ailments. One of the reasons that the autobiographical elements are so important in this novel is because Anaya is able to convey aspects of his own childhood that may not be considered true-to-life to readers not familiar with Mexican traditions. The mixture of folklore, religion, evil spirits, and superstition work to create a novel that resembles a romance novel. Antonio fights evil forces like the Trementina witches, who cast a deadly spell on his uncle; he experiences a magical moment with the golden carp; and he witnesses life in inanimate objects. Anaya's lyrical prose adds to the romantic and mysterious quality of the novel. The coming-of-age autobiographical novel is steeped in the power of *la tierra, la curandera* (the healer), and Catholicism. Above all, Anaya relies on landscape, on his sense of New Mexico, to convey the feelings of his characters. Landscape is crucial to Anaya's writing because, as he says, "My sense of place helps to define my center, and that center becomes the point of view from which I observe life" ("The Writer's Landscape" 100). The same becomes true for Antonio as he discovers, with the help of Ultima, that a profound understanding of landscape, combined with a harmonious spirituality, will allow him to resolve the conflict that haunts him throughout the novel.

Bless Me, Ultima (1972)

Bless Me, Ultima contains twenty-two chapters narrated retrospectively in the first person singular by Antonio Márez y Luna. The structure of the novel centers on two elements central to Anaya's concerns, the spiritual world and landscape. The novel moves in an episodic fashion, following Antonio's rite of passage from innocence, through crisis, to knowledge and self-awareness. The novel's action is also dictated by the four seasons. For example, the important events of the novel occur each summer: Ultima's arrival, Ultima's battle with evil, and Ultima's death. In this way Anaya successfully links *la tierra*, the earth or landscape, and its cycles to Antonio's journey, emphasizing that the seasons are directly linked to the inner self. The chapters between Ultima's arrival and death, the first and last chapters, portray the tensions and conflicts that plague Antonio in his spiritual search. The climax of the novel occurs at the center of the novel, the tenth chapter, when Ultima battles the evil spell that the Trementina daughters have cast on Antonio's Uncle Lucas. The final ten chapters portray the ensuing battle between Ultima and Tenorio, the father of the Trementina daughters, between good and evil.

The novel is centered on the conflict between dualities: the dualities are represented by El Puerto de los Lunas, or the farming land of the valley, and Las Pasturas, the *llano,* or the plains of the *vaqueros* (cowboys). On a spiritual level, the conflict, as interpreted by Antonio, is between Ultima and God—good versus evil, or myth (as in the golden carp and the mermaids) versus history. Antonio, between the ages of almost seven to nine, struggles with the belief that he must choose one or the other. He only sees the world in black and white, in dualistic Manichean terms. His coming-of-age is dependent on his realization that he can, and will, fuse elements. His question to Ultima illustrates his belief that he must choose: "Now we have come to live near the river, and yet near the llano. I love them both, and yet I am of neither. I wonder which life I will choose?" (*Bless Me, Ultima* 38). In the end, Ultima grants him the only lesson that will allow him to fuse the dualities that he faces, love.

Chapters 1 through 8 introduce the Márez y Luna family to Ultima, better known as *La Grande,* the great one, which means an old and wise woman who deserves respect. Ultima, who is old and alone, is provided for by the Márez y Luna family: "It was custom to provide for the old and the sick. There was always room in the safety and warmth of la familia for one more person" (*Bless Me, Ultima* 4).

Antonio lives with his parents and his sisters, Deborah and Theresa, in a small house in Guadalupe, situated just between his father's *llano* of Las Pasturas and his mother's farming village of El Puerto de los Lunas. Antonio's three older brothers, León, Andrew, and Eugene, are soldiers in World War II and do not return home until Chapter 7. Antonio is the son of two patriarchal clans that settled in New Mexico when it was still under Spanish rule. The two families represent the traditional Spanish families derived from: "The conquistador and the priest. The Márez are rough men that derive their symbolic name from seafaring conquistadors [Márez meaning mares/seas] turned sheepherders and vaqueros. . . . The Lunas derive their patronymic from a priest who founded a farming community in the valley of the moon" (Calderón "Chicano Narrative" 86). What characterizes both family ancestries is their connection to the earth, something that both parents miss. When the novel opens, Antonio's mother and father are dissatisfied, as they have been forced, largely because of their marriage, to abandon their way of life and their specific connection to the earth. Because they are alienated from their way of life, farming and sheepherding, they have been unable to pass along to Antonio and their other children any special connection to the land. Nevertheless, they pin their last hopes on Antonio, the youngest child. Antonio's mother wants him to become a farming priest, whereas his father wants him to become a *vaquero*.

Due to the burden of his parent's wishes, Antonio struggles with the belief that he must choose one way of life. His family's heritage pulls him in both directions. The dream Antonio has in Chapter 1 captures the conflict that can only be resolved through the natural world that Ultima teaches him to understand, respect, and love. In Antonio's dream of his own birth, his mother's family brings with them gifts from the earth, "fresh green chile and corn, ripe apples and peaches, pumpkins and green beans" (*Bless Me, Ultima* 5). In turn, when his father's family visits, they smash the gifts of fruit and replace them with "a saddle, horse blankets, bottles of whiskey, a new rope, bridles, chapas, and an old guitar" (*Bless Me, Ultima* 5). Antonio's mother wants nothing more than for Antonio to become a priest: "A community of farmers ruled over by a priest, she firmly believed, was the true way of life" (*Bless Me, Ultima* 27). His father, on the other hand, is not a strong believer in religion and, instead, wants "to gather his sons around him and move westward to the land of the setting sun, to the vineyards of California" (*Bless Me, Ultima* 13).

The family, though happy, is conflicted in many ways. Antonio is born in Las Pasturas, his father's land, the land of *vaqueros*. Antonio's mother is resentful that she has had to abandon her life as a farmer and live in Las Pasturas for many years. In turn, when she finally convinces Antonio's father to move, Gabriel feels resentment toward "she who kept him shackled to one piece of land" (*Bless Me, Ultima* 26). He is also bitter about the war taking away his three sons, and about having to abandon life as a *vaquero* to work, instead, on a highway that he will never use. He drinks, and he becomes drunk almost every Saturday; he "would rage against the town on the opposite side of the river which drained a man of his freedom" (*Bless Me, Ultima* 13).

The first chapter ends with the arrival of Ultima and her owl, which is the embodiment of her spirit. Although it is her arrival, Ultima knows that it also marks the end of her days. She tells Antonio, "I have come to spend the last days of my life here," to which Antonio responds, "You will never die,

Ultima . . . I will take care of you" (*Bless Me, Ultima* 11). Her arrival marks the beginning of the events that will change Antonio forever.

Antonio's loss of innocence begins in Chapter 2 when Lupito, a returned soldier from World War II who is mentally unbalanced because of the war, murders the town sheriff. The men of the town, including Antonio's father Gabriel, decide to find and kill Lupito. Antonio witnesses the townsmen shooting and killing Lupito. Traumatized by the incident, and questioning where Lupito's soul will go, Antonio returns home, where Ultima heals him for the first time. With Lupito's death comes a warning from Ultima's owl "that the time of peace on our hill [is] drawing to an end" (*Bless Me, Ultima* 14). In fact, Lupito's death will be followed by many more over the next two years, all of which occur after Chapter 10. Those who will die are Narciso, the town drunk, who tries to save Ultima from Tenorio; Florence, one of Antonio's friends who does not believe in God; Tenorio's daughters; Tenorio himself; and finally Ultima. The many deaths force Antonio to question God and the Catholic Church, heaven and hell, good and evil.

Chapters 3 through 9 offer portraits of the town, examine the role of the Catholic Church, and reveal Antonio's growing relationship with Ultima. Chapter 3 provides a portrait of the boys who live in the town and of Sunday Church. Chapter 4 takes place at the end of summer, the beginning of autumn, and depicts the yearly harvest of the Luna family. As is traditional, Antonio, his mother, and Ultima leave for the valley to help with the family harvest in the town of El Puerto. Upon his return from the harvest, Antonio begins school, entering the first grade. Chapter 7 introduces the reader to Antonio's brothers. Their arrival, which coincides with the end of World War II, occasions a change in the family. Gabriel Márez slowly realizes that his dream of building a new future in California, with his sons, has been destroyed by their encounter with the outside world. World War II serves as an historical event marking the change that will destroy the idyllic world of a small town in New Mexico.

Chapters 9, 10, and 11 are the heart of the novel, as they introduce folkloric elements that represent a way to interpret the world other than that provided by the Catholic Church. In Chapter 9, Antonio is told the story of how the golden carp became a god and how it is seen only once a year swimming in the river to the Hidden Lakes, where mermaids reside. The carp can only be seen by those initiated into a brotherhood that believes in the power of the earth and of water, of the natural world. Antonio is deemed old enough and special enough to be told the secret, and he is later taken to see the golden carp. In Chapter 10, Anaya accurately portrays an exorcism; Ultima battles the evil spell cast upon Antonio's Uncle Lucas by Tenorio's daughters, the Trementina witches. Chapter 10 also stands as Antonio's initiation into *curanderismo* (medicinal healing using cures made from local plants and herbs). Ultima's battle with evil depends on Antonio's innocence and strength and, thus, she employs him in his first *curandera* experience of real significance. Antonio's inherent goodness helps Ultima succeed where the Catholic Church failed, and Uncle Lucas survives. In Chapter 11, Antonio is finally taken to see the golden carp and, when he does, he experiences a moment of illumination: "This is what I had expected God to do at my first holy communion! If God was witness to my beholding of the golden carp then I had sinned!" (*Bless Me, Ultima* 105). These forces and elements of good expose the weaknesses of the Catholic Church, creating the core of questions that will haunt Antonio until the last chapter, in which he achieves a resolution.

The ensuing chapters detail both Antonio's initiation into Catholicism as he takes his first communion and his doubts about Catholicism, especially in light of the epic battle that takes place between Ultima and Tenorio, between good and evil. After saving Uncle Lucas, Ultima casts a spell on the three daughters, and they are killed. Ultima bewitches the three daughters because, as she tells Antonio, anyone who tampers with fate must be destroyed. Tenorio vows to avenge their deaths, and he pursues Ultima until he kills her in the final chapter of the novel. Chapter veintidós (twenty-two) is where Ultima (which means both "ultimate" and "the last"), dies, and Tenorio is killed, in turn, by Antonio's Uncle Pedro. It is the last summer of Antonio's childhood: "Sometimes when I look back on that summer I think that it was the last summer I was truly a child" (*Bless Me, Ultima* 238).

Interspersed throughout the narrative are Antonio's ten dreams. The first dream is that of his birth, and the last, in Chapter 22, is a reliving of the four deaths he has witnessed—Lupito's, Narciso's, Florence's, and Ultima's—the four good people who have died. This last is also a dream that destroys both the goodness of the church and the golden carp, as well as Ultima. Antonio's last cry in his dream is that of Jesus on the cross, "My God, my God, why have you forsaken me!" (*Bless Me, Ultima* 233).

Antonio's struggle centers on a dualism imposed on him by his mother and his father, by the Church and by his peers, by the fight between good and evil. Antonio will witness several episodes that will force him to reconsider his blind faith in what his parents want and in what the church wants. He will witness the deaths of Lupito, Narciso, and Florence, as well as a shamanic experience with Ultima, the horrors of Tenorio, and the evil force of the village. He will also become aware of his brother's sins. All of these experiences will force him to question the power of God versus that of Ultima, who heals Antonio's Uncle Lucas when the Church cannot. Antonio faces big questions: why does evil prevail, and why doesn't good conquer all? Ultima, more than either of his parents, is there throughout his coming-of-age, guiding him through the more difficult philosophical questions. In the end, Antonio endures several episodes that eventually give him, at the age of nine, a more holistic vision of the world; he accepts that he does not have to choose between two worlds. According to Anaya, "It seems to me that instead of a crucial episode there are many episodes that open Antonio's eyes until in the end he can begin to see, or perhaps see a glimmer of the truth which Ultima wanted him to see, and that is the holistic nature of the universe, to see beyond the dualities that at first are very apparent to him and those people he comes in contact with. Ultima asks him to see beyond that, to incorporate those dualities into a vision that is whole and into a vision that is complete" (Dash 52). For Ultima, good will always prevail over evil. Chapters 9, 10, and 11, the center of the narrative, illustrate this when Ultima battles the evil of Tenorio Trementina's *bruja* (witch) daughters. In using the innocent and good Antonio, Ultima battles evil and saves Uncle Lucas's life.

Antonio's spiritual journey indicates not only his loss of innocence, but also the loss of a way of life. Anaya juxtaposes Antonio's evolution with World War II and the dropping of the atomic bomb; both represent the end of an idyllic period. The women of the village proclaim, like a Greek chorus, that the atomic bomb is "a ball of white heat beyond the imagination, beyond hell," and they blame man. " 'Man was not made to know so much,' the old ladies cried in hushed, hoarse voices, 'they compete with God, they disturb the seasons, they seek to know more than God Himself. In the end, that knowledge they seek will destroy us all—' " (*Bless Me, Ultima* 183). New Mexico was the site of the first atomic bomb test, Antonio's brothers are fighting in World War II, and Anaya makes reference to the fact that almost everyone in the village has lost a son or husband in the war: "My mother and Ultima dressed in black because so many women of the town had lost sons or husbands in the war and they were in mourning" (*Bless Me, Ultima* 29). The return of Antonio's brothers marks the intrusion of the outside world on their small village. Eugene, León, and Andrew have witnessed good and evil in the war and return as men, no longer young boys willing to fulfill their father's dream. Despite this, Antonio will be able to maintain ties to the landscape, to the brotherhood of the golden carp, to *la Virgen* (the Virgin of Guadalupe), *la Llorona* (the "wailing woman" of Mexican legend), and the church. His conflicts are resolved only through Ultima's final belief that the purpose of one's life is to do good. Her final blessing, for which Antonio asks, conveys this belief: "I bless you in the name of all that is good and strong and beautiful, Antonio. Always have the strength to live. Love life, and if despair enters your heart, look for me in the evenings when the wind is gentle and the owls sing in the hills" (*Bless Me, Ultima* 247). This is the only time Antonio asks Ultima for a blessing, and it gives him the ability to understand the beauty and good in God, the golden carp and, most especially, in the landscape where Ultima resides. Along with Antonio's new understanding comes a new future, forever tied to *time* and the past, possessing elements of the lessons that he learned from Ultima.

CULTURAL ELEMENTS

Anaya's most important contribution in this novel is to introduce the reader to the landscape and history of New Mexico and to the archetype of Ultima, the *curandera*. The two are linked in the sense that, without an understanding of the landscape and the history, Ultima could not be understood. A *curandera*'s practices are rooted in the ancient religions of various Native American tribes, from the Pueblo to the Navajo. These tribes lived in the Southwest before the Spanish and then the Mexican conquests and colonizations. By paying tribute to the landscape, Anaya records the geographical location of some of the first Mexicans in the United States, and he celebrates their connection to both the Native American population and the Spanish explorers who settled the territory in the sixteenth century. With the inevitable racial mixing, the cultural traditions of the Native Americans were not erased; they have survived in contemporary society in combination with either Spanish or Mexican practices.

New Mexico first belonged to the Native Americans. When the Spaniards began to explore Nuevo México in the 1520s, they encountered these tribes. Racial mixing occurred and makes up much of the population today. New Mexico was first a colony of Spain and then of Mexico, after Mexico gained independence. The Mexican government desperately tried to populate the state with Mexicans who would retain allegiance to the central government in Mexico City. With this in mind, the newly formed Mexican government handed out land grants. The Luna family, from El Puerto de los Luna, is an example of one of the first families to settle the area. The history of El Puerto, the town from which Antonio's mother comes, is rooted in the 1800s: "The colony had first settled there under a land grant from the Mexican government, and the man who led the colonization was a priest, and he was a Luna" (*Bless Me, Ultima* 27). However, Mexico's rule was brief, ending with the victory of the United States in 1848. Under the rule of the United States, New Mexico remained relatively isolated until the introduction of the railroad in 1879, which not only connected New Mexico to the east but changed the face of its population. Until the advent of the railroad, New Mexico's population was mostly Spanish or *mestizo* (mixed race), but with the arrival of the railroad, more people began to move in from other parts of the United States. This created a state that would quickly adopt a social tier in which Native Americans and *mestizos* remained at the bottom. This is reflected in the disgruntled attitude of Antonio's father, Gabriel, who complains about working on a highway that he will never be able to use.

Anaya's novel stresses New Mexico's Spanish and Mexican heritage before it became a state in 1912. This Hispanic heritage, mixed with that of the indigenous peoples of the region, has created unique myths and traditions, some of which are portrayed in Anaya's novel. Folkways have also developed over the centuries: "For Nuevo Mexicanos of the valley, the heritage was the Spanish language, the Catholic religion, and the old folkways preserved by the farmers from villages like Puerto de Luna where my grandfather lived" (Anaya, *La Llorona* 50). In fact, throughout the novel, Anaya employs Spanish in the text without any translation. Whole sentences are sometimes incorporated into the narrative without any explanation. The reader who is not bilingual can still follow the plot, but Anaya makes no excuses and provides no translations for the bilingualism that exists throughout his novel. It is a tribute to the world in which he grew up and the world that continues to exist. As critics have noted, Spanish is no longer a foreign language. Like Anaya, Antonio's world is a bilingual world where Spanish is spoken by the older generations and Catholicism is practiced by all: "All of the older people spoke only in Spanish, and I myself understood only Spanish. It was only after one went to school that one learned English" (*Bless Me, Ultima* 9). Antonio's mother cherishes an expectation that Antonio will receive communion and become a priest. But his path toward priesthood is thwarted by the natural world that surrounds him and by its myths and folk beliefs.

Antonio encounters many cultural and folkloric elements on his journey that he attempts to interpret: *La Llorona*, the golden carp, mermaids, and *la Virgen de Guadalupe,* as well as historical and cultural practices of New Mexico, folkloric remedies, and more. *La Llorona* and *la Virgen de Guadalupe* are consistently mixed, as well, with stories from Ultima or the church. *La Llorona* and the golden carp are emblematic of childhood lore and folklore. *La Llorona,* also present in Cisneros's work, is typical of, but not exclusive to, Mexican Chicano folklore. Mexican culture worships *La Virgen de Guadalupe,* "the first dark Mestiza Virgin" (Rebolledo 50), who appeared before the Indian boy, Juan Diego, in 1531. Although the legend varies, some say Juan Diego was an old man, some a young Indian convert; some say that the Virgin made roses appear in a barren rocky hill, others in winter snow. What remains is that she has been adopted by the Mexican culture and stands as a syncretic figure. The name Guadalupe is "a possible rendering of the Aztec name Coatlaxopeuh, meaning 'she who has dominion over serpents.' Catholics believe this refers to how Guadalupe helped Christianity triumph over the serpents of Aztec paganism" ("Christian Legends in Cisneros' Work" 2; "The Guadalupe: Patroness of the Americas" 1). Regardless, the story of *la Virgen de Guadalupe* is passed down to all Catholic children. *La Virgen* is a source of strength, power, and hope. All Catholic children learn about the Virgin. Antonio's mother prays to *la Virgen* regarding every event of significance. Even Ultima prays to *la Virgen,* though she might not necessarily believe in her. Yet, she prays to her, recognizing her good powers and admiring them as she does the powers of all good forces, including her own.

However, Antonio is most powerfully influenced by Ultima, the *curandera* who learned "from the greatest healer of all time, the flying man from

Las Pasturas" (*Bless Me, Ultima* 80). As described by the narrator, "Ultima was a curandera, a woman who knew the herbs and remedies of the ancients, a miracle-worker who could heal the sick. And I had heard that Ultima could lift the curses laid by brujas, that she could exorcise the evil the witches planted in people to make them sick. And because a curandera has this power she was misunderstood and often suspected of practicing witch-craft herself" (*Bless Me, Ultima* 4).

The *curandera* is one of the most important archetypes in Chicano and Latino literature. A *curandera* is not only a healer; she is a *partera* (midwife) and a *bruja*. She embodies both positive and negative elements. She is a healer, but she also has the power to become a witch. Ultima never chooses to empower herself as a witch, although she is called *bruja* by Tenorio. Ultima quickly makes a distinction between herself and Tenorio's daughters, the Trementina sisters, who are the real *brujas* in Anaya's novel. A *bruja* will tamper with fate; a *curandera* only interferes with fate to lift evil curses. A *curandera* will not only call upon her own powers, but will also appeal to the Catholic Church since there are syncretic elements in *curanderismo*. The Catholicism brought by the Spanish settlers was combined with the tradi-tions of the Native Americans of the region. In Anaya's novel, the *curan-dera* never abuses her power and serves people only in the name of good.

The *curandera* can cure mental and physical illnesses with medicinal herbs and plants, but she can also lift curses. The most important examples of this in the novel are Ultima's battles with the evil spells cast upon Uncle Lucas in Chapter 10 and the Téllez family in Chapter 20. Unlike the local priest, in both cases Ultima is able to dispel the evil presence. Chapter 10 provides the most developed scene of witchcraft, describing not only the Black Mass but also how witches can travel in the form of fireballs, coyotes, and owls. In Chapter 10, the Trementina sisters are engaged in a Black Mass in honor of the devil, hoping to eventually dance with the devil. Lucas stumbles upon the dance and, being a Catholic, decides to give them a "Christian lashing" (*Bless Me, Ultima* 82). The witches attack Lucas and pull out his hair, which they later use to cast the evil spell. Both the Lucas and Téllez curses are called *mal puesto* (bewitchment) and, in both cases, priests from the church are the first people called in to help. The power of the priests' blessings are also thought to be able to exorcise evil forces. In the end, only Ultima is suc-cessful: "Only a *curandera* can diagnose a *mal puesto*. Only she can cure the victim, often with the use of black magic, prayers, herbal medicine, and their faith that God has given them special graces" (García and Holmes 5). Or, as in the case of Uncle Lucas, Antonio's pure Luna blood and his innocence are used to fight the evil curse. Ultima uses the innocence and goodness of his soul to battle the evil curse while his body channels the evil from Uncle Lucas. But Ultima also cures Antonio several times, either because he has experienced a *susto* (fright), as in Lupito's death, or because he suffers exhaustion after a shamanic experience Ultima may perhaps be the last *curandera* before the emergence of modern times. Her name means "last," and Anaya suggests that she is the last of her kind. The reference to the atomic bomb indicates the end of a way of life for all. Antonio will become the individual capable of fusing modern elements with the old traditions of the *curandera*. Only because she passed down stories and the power of the herbs, the presence of the river, the sound of the *llano*, to Antonio will her tradition survive. This is the most important theme that Anaya wants to convey. The past will survive through oral stories, and through individuals like Antonio, who are interested in the old ways, in traditions, and in myths, and who are young enough to accept Ultima without feeling threatened.

Ultima instills in Antonio an understanding and appreciation of the landscape of Nuevo Mexico and the traditions and history of yesteryear. Ultima follows the oral tradition that characterizes many of the homes of New Mexico, verbally passing down history, myths, and folklore to Antonio as they roam the landscape or visit in her room. Ultima is the connection that Antonio will always have with his past, and she is the future as well. Her teachings will continue to influence Antonio.

In the end, Anaya, who refuses to identify any single writer as an influence, claims the oral tradition of stories and folklore that are passed down, generation after generation, in the Southwest and the landscape of his childhood as such. In fact, Antonio believes that the *cuentos* (stories) he hears and the *tierra* (earth or landscape) that he learns about through Ultima mark the beginning of his journey toward a more holistic vision of the world and, especially, of the land on which he lives. The entire novel stands as a rich syncretic mixture of elements, from Catholicism to folklore. Easter Sunday is followed by a visit to the golden carp, and Antonio's holy communion becomes a meditation on the powers of other positive forces like Ultima.

FURTHER SUGGESTED READINGS

Works by Rudolfo Anaya

Anaya, Rudolfo. *Bless Me, Ultima*. New York: Warner Books, 1999.

———. *Shaman Winter*. New York: Warner Books, 1999.

———. *Maya's Children: The Story of La Llorona*. New York: Hyperion Books, 1997.

———. *Rio Grande Fall*. New York: Warner Books, 1997.

———. *Zia Summer*. New York: Warner Books, 1996.

———. *Albuquerque*. New York: Warner Books, 1994.

———. *Heart of Aztlán*. Albuquerque: University of New Mexico Press, 1988.

———. *Tortuga: A Novel*. Albuquerque: University of New Mexico Press, 1988.

Other Suggested Readings

Acosta, Oscar Zeta. *Autobiography of Brown Buffalo*. New York: Vintage, 1989.

Anaya, Rudolfo. "In Commemoration: *One Million Volumes.*" *The Magic of Words: Rudolfo A. Anaya and His Writings.* Ed. Paul Vassallo. Albuquerque: University of New Mexico Press, 1982.

Arias, Ron. *The Road to Tamazunchale.* Reno, NV: West Coast Poetry Review, 1975.

Calderón, Héctor. *Narratives of Greater Mexico: Essays on Chicano Literary History, Genre and Borders.* Austin: University of Texas Press (2004).

———. "To Read Chicano Narrative: Commentary and Metacommentary." *Mester* 11:2 (1983): 3–13.

"Christian Legends in Cisneros' Work." <geocities.com/SoHo/Workshop/4911/wgww/sandra/myths.html> p. 2. April 2002.

Garlarza, Ernesto. *Barrio Boy.* New York: Houghton Mifflin, 1992.

"The Guadalupe: Patroness of the Americas." <www.loveandmercy.org> p. 1. April 2002.

Hinojosa, Rolando. *Klail City.* Houston: Arte Público Press, 1987.

Rebolledo, Tey Diana. *Women Singing in the Snow: A Cultural Analysis of Chicana Literature.* Tucson and London: The University of Arizona Press, 1995.

Rechy, John. *The Miraculous Day of Amalia Gómez.* New York: Arcade Publishing, 1991.

Rivera, Tomás. *. . . Y no se lo tragó la tierra/ . . . and the Earth Did Not Devour Him.* Houston: Arte Público Press, 1987.

Villaseñor, José Antonio. *Pocho.* New York: Doubleday, 1970.

Chapter 3

The Fiction of Sandra Cisneros: The House on Mango Street *(1984) and* Woman Hollering Creek *(1991)*

S andra Cisneros was born in Chicago, Illinois, in 1954 and currently resides in San Antonio, Texas. Born of a Mexican father and a Mexican American mother, Cisneros has never forgotten her roots. She dedicated *Woman Hollering Creek* (1991) to her mother, who gave Cisneros a "fierce language," and to her father, who gave her "el lenguaje de la ternura/the language of tenderness" (*Woman Hollering Creek* Acknowledgements). The fierce Chicago English and the tender Mexican Spanish that filled her household as a child are part of her prose in both her fiction and poetry. Cisneros's combination of languages is matched by the cultural mixture of the Anglo and Mexican worlds, of *La Virgen de Guadalupe* and the Alamo, of Jackie Kennedy and *la frontera* (the border). Cisneros, like members of many border families, has characterized her family as "a commuter family" (Kevane and Heredia 46), always moving between Chicago and Mexico during the fifties and sixties. Her novel *Caramelo* is based on the traveling back and forth across the border. Taken together, these elements—the mix of languages and cultures, and the travel back and forth across the border—highlight the differences that Cisneros had to weigh and balance on a daily basis as a Latina American/Chicana Mexican in the United States.

Cisneros describes her childhood as a young girl in a Latino *barrio* of Chicago as sheltered and protected, that of a "princess" (Kevane and Heredia 49). Despite the poverty, the gangs, and the lack of opportunities,

Cisneros survived her surroundings. Her mother allowed her the luxury of reading, and her parents made sure she received a solid education. Although given these opportunities, she was expected to stay with her family in Chicago, to marry, and to become a mother, like a traditional Mexican Catholic daughter. However, Cisneros successfully avoided this tradition. After graduating from Loyola University in 1976, she attended graduate school at the Iowa Writers' Workshop. Here, she not only discovered how different her upbringing had been from many of her peers, but she also experienced her first taste of freedom. She became determined not to become somebody's wife or mother. She says that she has managed to defy the heavy Mexican Catholic pressure to marry and become a mother because she "had huevos [courage]! I had ganas [the desire] because I knew I was not going to stay in my father's house. I had just come back from graduate school. I had tasted freedom and I liked it!" (Kevane and Heredia 50).

When Cisneros graduated from the Iowa Writers' Workshop in 1978, she left with a manuscript that would later become *The House on Mango Street*. However, this book was not published until 1984. At the time she was enrolled in the workshop, Cisneros imitated voices that did not capture her own experiences. Eventually, after leaving the workshop, she realized that she needed to write about her own experiences. During those six years, Cisneros returned to her Latino community in the sense that she dedicated herself to working with Latino students, high-school dropouts, pregnant teenagers, and others. In many ways, *The House on Mango Street* parallels Cisneros's own journey from an urban Latino neighborhood to her role as a social advocate. In a recent interview, Cisneros states, "I was forming my spirituality and my politics at the time that Esperanza was. If you had asked me these questions at the time I was writing it, I would not have been able to articulate it as spiritual and political. I just knew that I was moved by things I was learning as I was working in the community. As I learned those lessons, they emerged in my text. I was just writing from my heart" (Kevane and Heredia 49). In her heart, Cisneros felt anger and outrage and a certain sense of responsibility. Compared to the young people with whom she worked, she had led a privileged life. The disparity between her life and that of the youth who surrounded her compelled Cisneros to write stories for those who remain invisible in society, those who are unable to record their lives and experiences, those who don't have a voice. Cisneros's journey toward this political, spiritual, and social awareness parallels that of her protagonist Esperanza Cordero. Like Cisneros, Esperanza would probably not qualify her transformation as such, yet it is linked to an emerging political, social, and spiritual awareness of the individual's debt to his or her community. Each of their journeys resist Cisneros's shame and denial about one's heritage and identity. Instead, it embraces and empowers the self, including mixed roots and a feminine identity.

After *The House on Mango Street,* Cisneros published her second collection of poems, *My Wicked Wicked Ways* (1987), her second collection of stories *Woman Hollering Creek* (1991), and another collection of poetry, *Loose Woman* (1994). Prior to these works, a chapbook of poems, *Bad Boys,* was published by Mango Publications in 1980. Cisneros's poetry and prose are heavily linked together. For example, Cisneros has stated that *My Wicked Wicked Ways* is the more autobiographical work, although linked to *Mango Street.* It would be useful to read her poems in light of her stories, as similar themes and characters will be found. Perhaps because of the passion of her work, Cisneros has become a highly celebrated Chicana author. She has successfully created a loyal following of readers, who are drawn to her work because they feel validated when they see their experiences in print. Currently, Cisneros lives in a purple house in San Antonio, Texas, and serves as a spokesperson for many Chicano and Latino issues. Though she admits that this takes away from her writing—for example, it has taken ten years to complete *Caramelo,* or *Puro cuentos* (2002)—she sees it as her responsibility. Her work represents an effort begun in the eighties and shared by other Latina writers, such as Gloria Anzaldua, Cherríe Moraga, Helena María Viramontes, to describe the life of Latinas in the United States. Cisneros began to write as a way to record the community in which she lived. Serving as interpreter, amphibian, cartographer, or mediator—all words she has used to describe her role as writer—Cisneros's writing attempts to bridge two world cultures, American and Mexican.

The House on Mango Street, published originally by Arte Público Press, was so well received that Vintage Press reissued the collection in 1989. Cisneros's collection had definitely struck a chord with both Latino and American audiences because it combined the coming-of-age story with Latino, specifically Mexican American, cultural issues. The stories trace the changes in Esperanza Cordero, a young innocent girl who will arrive at a profound knowledge and awareness of her surroundings and of what her future will be. Esperanza literally becomes a writer who will record the stories of those who cannot tell their stories, of those, as the collection says, who "cannot out." Cisneros's major contribution to the traditional *bildungsroman,* the story of a young protagonist who gains awareness, is that the evolution of her character takes place in the invisible *barrio,* the neighborhood that people are afraid to enter, where poverty prevails. Self-knowledge and self-realization are experienced by a young girl in a "brown" neighborhood.

The House on Mango Street (1984)

The House on Mango Street is a collection of forty-four stories that describe Esperanza Cordero and her poor neighborhood in Chicago. Esperanza, the oldest of the Cordero family, has two brothers, Carlos and Kiki, and a younger sister, Nenny. Although we never know exactly how old she is, we do know she is younger than some of the characters in the collection—for example Alicia, who is a freshman in college, and Marin, who is perhaps fifteen or sixteen. Esperanza is probably in the seventh or eighth grade since, in the story "The First Job," she says she needs to work because the Catholic high school is expensive. This implies that she is either headed to high school or is in the ninth grade. However, because of the language of the narrative and her experiences, one can assume that Esperanza is about thirteen years old.

The forty-four stories vary in length, from one sentence ("A House of My Own") and two paragraphs to four and a half pages, the longest story in the book. Because of the brevity of these stories, there has been much discussion about the genre of this work. Some have called it a novel, some stories, some vignettes, some poetry. Nevertheless, if the reader examines the forty-four stories as a whole, a strong story line is discovered that traces the coming-of-age of Esperanza Cordero. Each story is told from the point of view of a young girl attempting to understand her own identity. The stories describe both Esperanza's inner world and the world of the *barrio* in which she lives. From both of these inner monologues, and from her observations and interactions with the members of her community, Esperanza will return to her community as a socially aware writer.

Two narrative threads connect the stories in *The House on Mango Street*: the personal and private story of Esperanza Cordero, and the public and collective story of the neighborhood on Mango Street. Cisneros presents us with a Latino *barrio* of impoverished, struggling individuals who strive to better themselves, but who are mostly trapped by cultural or social oppression. Stories of immigrants, like "Geraldo No Last Name" and "No Speak English" reveal the difficulties faced by the Latino population as they move north in search of employment or to be reunited with family. Stories of women staring out of windows or having too many babies, trapped indoors because of jealous husbands, and unable to speak English, reveal both their fear of the dominant culture and the oppression of the patriarchal system.

Esperanza's personal transformation is rooted in her observations about the people in her neighborhood, which provide her with a community education. From each member of her community, she will learn what to become and what not to become. For the most part, Esperanza learns her lessons from *las mujeres* (the women), to whom Cisneros dedicated the collection. The dedication to the *mujeres* attests to Cisneros's desire to recognize and acknowledge the difficult path that Latina women face, especially when they choose to better themselves. Cisneros worked with many young pregnant girls, with women and girls who were abused by husbands or fathers, and with women who had no options because they were saddled with children. Esperanza's coming-of-age is largely a struggle to sift through the role models and peers who surround her and to emerge as a success. A core group of stories describe the women who offer Esperanza advice, advice that she does not understand in the narration of the story but that she will understand as author of the stories we read. The stories alternate between Esperanza's realization that she will not, or cannot, stay in her neighborhood lest she suffer the fate of most of the girls around her, and the descriptions of the *barrio* itself. Esperanza's final realization is that she will leave but that she will return through the written word: "I have gone away to come back. For the ones I left behind. For the ones who cannot out."

Instead of offering the plot of each story, this analysis will present the forty-four stories divided into two helpful categories, the stories that contribute to Esperanza's transformation, and the stories that describe the *barrio*. The stories that are directly relevant to Esperanza can be grouped as follows: "The House on Mango Street," "My Name," "Those Who Don't," "A Rice Sandwich," "Hips," "The First Job," "Papa" "Born Bad," "Elenita, Cards, Palm and Water," "Four Skinny Trees," "Bums in the Attic," "Beautiful & Cruel," "A Smart Cookie," "The Three Sisters," "Alicia & I," "A House of My Own," and "Mango Says Goodbye Sometimes." Taken together, these stories contain Esperanza's dreams about her future; thoughts about herself; advice from important female role models; and her final realization about her home, which is in her heart, and her place as a Latina Mexican woman in the United States.

"The House on Mango Street," the first story of the collection, specifies the commuter nature of Esperanza's family who, like many people of a lower socioeconomic class, move frequently, either seeking a better living arrangement or because they cannot afford the rent. Esperanza is tired of apartments and homes with broken water pipes and crooked steps. She is ashamed of the poverty that haunts her family, of the shabby homes in which they live. Esperanza projects her feelings of shame and embarrassment about her family's poverty upon her house. With the shame comes Esperanza's strong dream of having a home of her own, a real house, she says, with a basement and a washroom, a white house with a big yard "like the houses on T.V." It will be a house from which she will derive pride, "One I could point to" (*Mango Street* 5). The idea of house and home parallels Esperanza's feelings about her identity; her first dream of a house marks the beginning of Esperanza's journey, during which not only will her idea of a house be transformed, but also her identity. If at first Esperanza imagines an artificial house to be emblematic of success and self-confidence, at the end of the story, the house evolves into one that reflects Esperanza's sense of community and pride in her roots. Her final vision of a house of her own includes not only writing tools and solitude, but also the "bums" who will sleep in the attic.

"My Name" reveals Esperanza's cultural heritage. The story describes Esperanza's great-grandmother from Mexico, from whom she inherited her name. Esperanza means both "a hope" and "to wait," from the verb *esperar*.

Her great-grandmother was an independent, strong woman, "so wild she wouldn't marry," says Esperanza. But, given Mexican tradition, she was forced into a marriage as if she were a piece of property, or, as Esperanza says, "as if she were a fancy chandelier" (*Mango Street* 11). The story of the great-grandmother illustrates the patriarchal system that characterizes Mexican culture, mainly that women should marry, have children, and remain housewives. These gender models have been defied by Cisneros herself, who has remained "nobody's mother, nobody's wife." Denial of the traditional gender role is seen as a betrayal of Mexican culture. Esperanza will reject one part of her grandmother's captivity tale: she vows not to live her life *esperando* (waiting) on a windowsill. Rather, she *espera* (hopes) that she will inherit the wild, independent side of her great-grandmother. (The only other female character in the novel who refuses to fully adopt the traditional female role is Esperanza's friend, Alicia, who pursues a university education. At the same time, however, Alicia also makes tortillas and keeps house for her father.) Esperanza links her cultural heritage to her desire to create a new name, to reinvent herself as someone who will not be captured and married, someone whose name represents this wildness, like "Zeze the X," a fanciful name where the X represents many possibilities of reinvention.

"Those Who Don't" and "A Rice Sandwich" communicate the fear and shame that accompany poverty. In "Those Who Don't," Esperanza describes her neighborhood and how it is perceived by outsiders. Her *barrio,* though feared by outsiders, mainly Anglos, is "All brown all around" and, according to Esperanza, "safe." However, the Anglos' fear is also felt by inhabitants of her brown neighborhood when they venture into other neighborhoods of color. The place of African Americans and Latinos on the social hierarchy has long been a source of conflict: Latinos are afraid of African Americans, Anglo Americans are afraid of Latinos and, as Esperanza observes, "That is how it goes and goes" (*Mango Street* 28).

In "A Rice Sandwich," Esperanza wants to eat in the canteen with the "special kids" who live far away and can't go home for lunch. But, when Esperanza is about to get in line, a nun notices her and does not allow her to enter. Instead, the nun forces her to see the Sister Superior, who makes Esperanza "stand up on a box of books and point. That one? She said pointing to a row of ugly three-flats, the ones even the raggedy men are ashamed to go into. Yes, I nodded even though I knew that wasn't my house and started to cry" (*Mango Street* 45). The nun assumes that Esperanza, because of her ethnic heritage, lives in a run-down house; she demeans and categorizes her. Cisneros sensitively portrays a young child's feelings and also criticizes the religious school Esperanza attends, an institution that fails to instill a sense of pride about their ethnic origins in children of color.

The five stories near the center of the novel, "Hips," "The First Job," "Papa Who Wakes Up Tired in the Dark," "Born Bad," and "Elenita, Cards, Palm, Water," reveal impending physical, social, and mental changes in

Esperanza. "Hips" symbolizes the physical maturation of Esperanza. As Esperanza tells her friends, "One day you wake up and they are there. Ready and waiting like a new Buick with the keys in the ignition. Ready to take you where?" The growing of hips marks a physical change, girls on the verge of becoming women, whereas the question that Esperanza asks marks a mental change with regard to the future and its possibilities. Are these young girls to use their hips to have children? Now that they have hips, are they to marry? To become wives, mothers, housewives? The question "To where?" will be answered by the women who offer Esperanza advice. The story "First Job" also marks a new maturity and sense of responsibility and indicates that Esperanza must join the workforce out of economic necessity. Joining the workforce has an important significance as well because the role of most Latina women of color in the workforce has been that of factory or garment worker, nanny, or other jobs that are not part of the capitalistic society that represents the American dream. Esperanza enters the workforce only to have her job end quickly when an older man preys upon her, taking advantage of her age and innocence, kissing her forcefully. With growing mental maturity, there is a physical change that marks the danger of sexuality and of becoming an object to men. "Papa Who Wakes Up Tired" also reveals Esperanza's growing maturity. Her father tells her about his father's death. The fact that he tells her and that he cries in front of her reveals to Esperanza her role as the oldest daughter. In addition, it forces her to face the mortality of her own father.

In the next two stories, Esperanza is offered her first pieces of advice. At this stage in her development, she will not know how to interpret the advice. However, toward the end of the collection, this advice will form a precious key that will help unlock her future and will allow her to free herself from the restraints of her community. "Born Bad" explores Esperanza's relationship with her dying aunt. The importance of this story is not the games she plays with her friends while visiting her Aunt Lupe, but the time she spends alone with her aunt. Aunt Lupe enjoys when Esperanza reads to her. One day Esperanza reads one of her own poems, and her aunt tells her to remember to keep writing. In an environment in which education and literacy is a luxury, Esperanza's aunt recognizes the opportunities that reading and writing can offer. In "Elenita," Esperanza visits a "witch woman" to hear her future. The mix of Catholic and pagan elements, found on Elena's refrigerator—holy candles, a plaster saint, a Palm Sunday cross, and a picture of the voodoo hand—are contrasted with the sounds of the television that Elena's son is watching. Elena, amidst the noise of her home, amidst the mix of two worlds, offers Esperanza, "A home in the heart[.] . . . A house made of heart" (*Mango Street* 64).

"Four Skinny Trees" and "Bums in the Attic" demonstrate Esperanza's growing awareness of her surroundings and her desire to derive strength from them. In "Four Skinny Trees," Esperanza understands that the trees have strength, especially as they thrive in an area that is not favorable to growth. The four trees, that grow "despite concrete," symbolize Esperanza herself: she will grow despite the odds against her. "Bums in the Attic," in turn, demonstrates a sense of humor and pride. Esperanza dreams of a house in a rich area, but she will never forget about "those of us who live too much on earth" (86). When she owns her own house, she vows not to forget where she came from and to offer "bums" a place to stay. While Esperanza's sense of social justice is emerging, so is her sense of her female identity. After observing the women of her *barrio*—most trapped, abused, and virtually imprisoned by husbands and fathers, and by lack of opportunities— Esperanza declares war. In "Beautiful & Cruel," Esperanza knows what it means to be a daughter of a Mexican father. She decides to start her own war, in which she will not be subjected to traditional gender roles. "The importance of this lies in her blatant declarations and conscious choices. To speak as "I" instead of placing the family first, demonstrates Esperanza's res- olution not to become entrapped like "A Smart Cookie." This next story is told from her mother's point of view, who also speaks to the traditional role of women in a Mexican household. Esperanza's own mother tells her that shame is bad. Her mother tells her this because she herself felt shame about her clothes, as Esperanza does about her home. Most likely, her mother understands that Esperanza needs guidance. Instead of telling her to learn how to cook, wash, and clean, she tells her: "Esperanza, you go to school. Study hard" (*Mango Street* 91). School is Esperanza's way out; otherwise, she will end up like Madam Butterfly, or like her mother's *comadres,* (very close family friends) whose husbands have left or died.

Just as there are five core stories at the center of the collection, the last four stories form another core and point to what Esperanza will become and what her future will be. In "The Three Sisters," we meet Lucy and Rachel's aunts or *comadres,* who arrive because Lucy and Rachel's baby sister has died. Esperanza describes their arrival as almost mythical, and the sisters as related to the moon. At the wake, Rachel's aunts, the three sisters, pick out Esperanza as the special one and allow her one wish. After Esperanza makes a wish, one of the three pulls her aside and tells her to always remember her roots, to never forget Mango Street. Because of her advice, we understand that Esperanza's wish is to leave the *barrio* and never return. Although she feels embarrassed at having her selfish wish discovered, she will not forget the gentle admonition of the woman.

The last three stories of this group reiterate what the three sisters tell her. "Alicia & I Talking on Edna's Steps" takes place at least one year after Esperanza has moved into 4006 Mango Street. When Esperanza complains that she is not proud of her house, Alicia tells her, "Like it or not you are Mango Street, and one day you'll come back" (*Mango Street* 107). The story that follows, "A House of My Own," provides a definition of the kind of home Esperanza desires. Now her dream house has less to do with the physical appearance of a home and more to do with freedom and wildness, books and stories, a space for herself—not a father's or a husband's home, but one all her own.

Finally, in "Mango Says Goodbye Sometimes" the reader discovers that Esperanza has internalized all of the advice and experiences from that year. She will keep writing because writing takes the "ghost" away; she will leave because she is strong enough to return: "I have gone away to come back. For the ones I left behind. For the ones who cannot out" (*Mango Street* 110). The story has come full circle, and Esperanza has become the writer, the recorder of her neighborhood, offering hope to all those who cannot tell their stories and who have no voice. "Born Bad," "Beautiful & Cruel," "A Smart Cookie," "Elenita, Card, Palm, Water," "The Three Sisters," and "Alicia & I," are all stories of women who see something special in Esperanza and who offer her advice, the only gift they can give this young girl. These pieces of advice offer Esperanza a way to interpret and internalize her identity in a positive way. And, as shall be seen, she will leave Mango Street with a sense of loyalty toward her community and her roots. The desire for a physical home evolves into a spiritual and political home, one that will allow Esperanza freedom, but will allow her to remain loyal to her *barrio,* and one that will emerge through the written word. In effect, *The House on Mango Street* is the house of stories through which Esperanza/Cisneros gives voice to her neighborhood. Her journey is accomplished.

THE *BARRIO*

As stated before, Esperanza's journey is deeply rooted in her observations about her barrio. They aid her in coming to terms with her identity. Esperanza's search for her identity and her coming-of-age is universal; most readers will be able to identify with the feelings that trouble Esperanza—feelings of not belonging, of being other, of "the shame of being poor, of being female, of being not-quite-good-enough," as Cisneros states in the introduction to the tenth-anniversary edition (1993). The answer to these feelings, according to Cisneros, is to recover, celebrate, and always remember one's roots. In this respect, *The House on Mango Street* not only records Esperanza's story, but that of her *barrio.* Cisneros gives voice to the historically silenced members of the community. Esperanza records, as a writer, her own personal journey toward transformation, but also that of her neighborhood, a neighborhood that represents the collective story of Latino neighborhoods across the United States. Esperanza seeks to discover and clarify her identity through the members of her community—Mexicans, Puerto Ricans, Central Americans, legal and illegal immigrants, native people of color. The depiction of the *barrio* contains the collective themes of poverty, racism, migration, and patriarchy, and the subsequent destruction that they create in the community. Cisneros paints portraits of different characters, almost all trapped victims of social or patriarchal restrictions. Women withdraw behind locked doors and windows, and young men and women struggle to find meaning and validation in their *barrio* and in the world outside their neighborhood.

Cathy in "Cathy Queen of Cats" introduces the reader and Esperanza to the people in the neighborhood. When Esperanza and her family move in, Cathy, whose family is moving out, reveals that her own family is moving because the neighborhood is going downhill; Latinos like Esperanza and other people of color are moving in. The "neighborhood is getting bad" (13), she states. The fact that the narrator and Cathy are so young allows for these kinds of conversations, in which ethnic and racial differences are discussed in a matter-of-fact manner. As Cathy and Esperanza talk, Cathy describes everyone in the neighborhood. The neighborhood contains danger: Joe, the baby-grabber; Benny and Blanca, the corner store owners; and Edna, "the lady who owns the building next to you." Cathy also gives Esperanza advice about whom to befriend and whom not to befriend. She tells Esperanza not to become friends with Lucy and Rachel, whom she describes as "Two girls raggedy as rats." She tells Esperanza to stay away from Alicia, who has become "stuck-up" because she is in college.

After Cathy introduces the neighborhood, we are presented with several different portraits of the female members of the community. "There Was an Old Woman She Had so Many Children She Didn't Know What to Do" is a play on the old Mother Goose rhyme, "There Was an Old Lady Who Lived in a Shoe." Although the Mother Goose story also speaks of poverty, it does so in a whimsical manner. In turn, Cisneros's story reels from the poverty and many children that form the life of Rosa Vargas, "who cries every day for the man who left without even leaving a dollar for bologna" (*Mango Street* 29). Rosa Vargas also cries every day because she has too many children, and she is too tired to take care of them. She has so many children that she cannot watch them, and her son Angel dies from flying out a window "like a sugar donut, just like a falling star, and exploded down to earth without even an 'Oh' " (*Mango Street* 30). Alicia, the character in "Alicia Who Sees Mice," is motherless and afraid of mice, and perhaps of her father, the story suggests. Although she attends the university, she still must wake up early to make tortillas for her father. Mamacita in "No Speak English" arrives in the United States after her husband struggled to save money to bring her over. Mamacita never learns English and remains inside the apartment pining for her homeland. In "Rafaela Who Drinks Coconut & Papaya Juice on Tuesdays," Rafaela is young and married but is weary and trapped. Sally, in the story of the same name, is too beautiful. Her father tells her that being beautiful is trouble and, being "very strict in his religion" (81), he hits her frequently so she doesn't turn out like his sisters who, when he remembers them, make him sad. Of all the female characters in the collection, Esperanza feels a special affinity toward Sally and imagines a new home for her. Esperanza sees a home for Sally where the windows "would swing open"; all the sky would come in, where she could love without censure (82–83). Finally, there is Minerva, who writes poems but who is already married with two kids and a husband who has left her and keeps leaving, and who abuses her as well. Esperanza observes the vicious cycle—Minerva letting her husband continue to return, but also the fact that "her daughters will go that way too" (*Mango Street* 84).

There are portraits of young boys in the *barrio* as well. "Meme Ortiz," whose real name is Juan, moves into Cathy's house and breaks both arms jumping off a tree. "Louie, His Cousin & His Other Cousin," is the story of a Puerto Rican family. Louie's cousin steals a big yellow Cadillac, gives the neighborhood children a ride in it, and is caught by the police and taken away. The story demonstrates the abrupt end to Louie's cousin, who will most likely be placed in one juvenile detention center after another. "Geraldo No Last Name" describes an immigrant *bracero* (farm worker) who arrives in the United States seeking employment in order to send money home to his family. Geraldo, as described by the narrator, is "just another *brazer* (also a farm worker; English slang for *bracero*) who didn't speak English. Just another wetback" (*Mango Street* 66). Cisneros, however, provides the reader with a background for Geraldo, who arrives in the United States as a young boy, seen as invisible and without a history of any importance by the dominant class. Geraldo travels north, like so many other immigrants from Mexico, Central America, and South America, to financially help his family by sending money home every week. However, after being hit by a car, he is virtually left to die in the hospital. His family will most likely never discover what happened to him. Cisneros highlights the hospital staff's callousness toward Geraldo, just as she did the nun's callousness toward Esperanza. The surgeon never comes, the intern is not interested in aiding Geraldo because he has no name and, therefore, he is not important. By recording this story, Cisneros attempts to give Geraldo a history and a story, so that he becomes memorable as a person. Cisneros shows the callousness of society toward an illegal immigrant, but she includes Geraldo's story to demonstrate that we might have it all wrong. Someone seen as just another *bracero,* an immigrant worker who does not deserve medical care and who is left to die alone, is actually a hard-working man who is hoping to help his family survive.

Throughout these stories, we witness the people who make up the *barrio,* the invisible immigrants and the legal residents who are segregated because of color, race, or economic status. Many of these *barrio* portraits reveal the prejudice and misunderstanding prevalent in North American attitudes toward Latino communities. Each one of these stories gives voice to these problems on an emotional level so that we can identify with the characters and their struggle to survive in a foreign and, oftentimes, hostile environment. The creation of the *barrio* characters pays tribute to Cisneros's roots. The *barrio* is Esperanza's place of origin and, thus, synonymous with the origins of her identity. Esperanza observes, in both subtle and not so subtle forms, patriarchal oppression, domestic abuse, sexism, intolerance, oppression, bigotry, and poverty. Her sense of self will be derived from these observations; she realizes that she can potentially become any of the women she observes. That she survives, like the four skinny trees outside her window, is tribute to her strength, the strength of a young girl who already knows she does not want to inherit a place by the window. The collective community that surrounds her functions as a chorus of voices. They present her with advice, and they show her the potential dangers facing a young Mexican American girl on the verge of womanhood. Esperanza would not have remembered and returned to her roots without the voices of the other members of her community.

Woman Hollering Creek and Other Stories (1991)

The stories that form *The House on Mango Street* are geographically anchored in Chicago, in a Latino *barrio* on Mango Street, seen from the locus of Esperanza's house. With *Woman Hollering Creek and Other Stories,* Cisneros moves to *la frontera* (the border) between Mexico and the United States. The twenty-two stories that make up her second collection move back and forth between the cities that line the almost 2,500 mile-long border between the two countries. *El otro lado,* or "the other side," a prevalent term in this collection, refers to either side of the border, depending on where the characters are situated. The Mexican American border-town communities have family on both sides and, depending on circumstances—such as teenage pregnancy, domestic abuse, or visiting family members—the characters in this collection will remake a home on either side of the border. In addition, unlike the stories in *The House on Mango Street,* each of these stories contains a different narrator; this adds to the quality of displacement that characterizes the natural and transient movement across the border. In fact, border crossing is so prevalent in this collection that, at times, it is difficult to pinpoint the exact location of the story. Cisneros chose this fluid narrative tactic in order to emphasize the movement and travel that characterize Mexicans, Chicanos, and Mexican Americans.

Esperanza Cordero provided us with a *bildungsroman* of a young Latina girl, and with issues of acculturation that accompany a bicultural coming-of-age. *Woman Hollering Creek* provides us with many portraits of different Chicana/Latina types and reveals how they balance their Mexican traditions with their contemporary status in the United States. In this collection, Cisneros explores different types of Chicana experiences of border life. She feels that it is her responsibility to "represent the entire spectrum of our community" (Kevane and Heredia 52). What is most notable and enriching in this collection, however, is Cisneros's return to important Mexican arche-types, ancient cultural traditions, and defining events in Mexican history. Cisneros explores how these ancient traditions, myths, and history affect the characters on both sides of the border: the characters engage with *la Virgen de Guadalupe de Tonitzín,* la Malinche, Mexican movies, Mayan gods and legends, myths like that of *La Llorona,* el Príncipe Popo, the Alamo, the Mexican Revolution, and *curanderas* and *brujas.* Through her characters, Cisneros demonstrates how Mexico's cultural traditions have come to bear on the contemporary Mexican American individual.

Woman Hollering Creek is divided into three parts that imitate the three stages of life for a Chicana Mexican Latina (Calderón, "Cisneros's Feminist Border Stories" 50). Part I of the collection contains stories that portray the innocence of childhood, the obsession with playing and having a best friend, and the origins of the bicultural and bilingual identity that will find expres-sion in the female characters in Parts II and III. Part I portrays familial love and security; Part II explores adolescence and provides an introduction to teenage attractions and love between the sexes; Part III focuses on gender issues, marriage, motherhood, being single, and the complicated relation-ships between men and women, especially when women are trying to define themselves in a patriarchal world.

Part I, "My Friend Lucy Who Smells Like Corn," contains seven stories. The first six stories are told in the same childlike voice found in *The House on Mango Street.* However, the last story, "Tepeyac," is narrated from an adult's point of view. The stories in Part I, with the exception of "Tepeyac," reveal the innocent concerns that characterize a child's world: the best friend; the comfort, warmth, and security of family; the extended family; birthdays; moments of shame; play with Barbies; and more. The seven sto-ries are different from those in Cisneros's first collection in that they employ more cultural signifiers and Spanish. For example, "My Friend Lucy," is full of the five senses, smells, taste, touch, sight, and sounds through which the young girls interpret the world. We learn that Lucy's hair smells like *nix-matal,* a Nahúatl word that means a mixture of ground corn and lime for tortillas. Cisneros does not translate Spanish or indigenous words, but leaves them in order to connote the Mexican and indigenous influences that exist in the homes of these *mestizo* families. Lucy's siblings' names reflect their bicultural background. Some siblings have English names, like Nancy and Amber Sue, and some have Spanish names, like Ofelia and Herminia.

The last two stories are the most important in terms of their themes: bilin-gual and bicultural identity, crossing the border, and knowing or not know-ing that one's home lies in two countries. "Mericans" plays with the border identity, whereas "Tepeyac" is a story about recognizing, longing for, and returning to one's roots. The title "Mericans" is significant to the story in that it plays on the names of both countries, Mexico and America, 'Me' for Mexico and 'Mericans' the latter part of America. The story describes three grandchildren waiting for their grandmother, who is inside *La Basílica* praying for the souls of her family members. All three grandchildren, "born in that barbaric country with its barbarian ways" (19), as the grandmother refers to the United States, have double names that reflect their double identities. On the American side of the border, they are Michelle, Junior, and Keeks; on the other side, with their *abuela* (grandmother), they are called by their Mexican names, Micaela, Enrique, and Alfredito. The doubleness is carried on throughout the story. The church in which the *abuela* prays is all "dust and dark" inside, signifying the past—holy and ancient. No one in the *abuela*'s family prays anymore, so she prays for all of her children and grandchildren. Outside it is bright and hot, and Keeks is playing games that reflect American pop culture—Flash Gordon, the Lone Ranger, and other superhero figures. The *abuela* is seen as awful because she prays and speaks to them in Spanish. She is awful, in a sense, because she represents an old, strict, traditional religious Mexican family. Just as Micaela/Michelle calls her grandmother awful, the grandmother, perhaps, sees her granddaughter the same way—for not speaking Spanish properly, for not behaving properly, and for having been born in that "barbaric country." The ending brings the duality of the story together, when tourists see the children and think that they are cute little Mexican kids. They want to take back a souvenir of the Mexican child sitting against a Mexican church. The irony, of course, is that the children respond in English, surprising the American tourists, as they yell out, over and over again, "We're Mericans, we're Mericans" (*Woman Hollering* 20).

"Tepeyac," in turn, continues in the same religious vein as the previous story, and might even contain the same praying *abuela*. The story, about a young girl who walks home with her grandfather every day from his *tlapalería* (hardware store), ends with the memories of the now-adult woman who returns and revisits her grandparents' home in Tepeyac. Cisneros's own grandparents lived in Tepeyac, at calle La Fortuna 12 (Fortune 12). It is likely that the story's narrator is Cisneros's alter ego since, at one point, the narrator recognizes the shape of her initials in the green iron gate of her grandparents' home. Her description of the "arabesque and scroll like the initials of my name" (*Woman Hollering* 23) suggests the curls and curves of the letters "S and C."

Tepeyac is an historically important town on the outskirts of Mexico City, where Juan Diego, an Indian peasant, encountered *La Virgen de Guadalupe* on December 9, 1531. The legend tells that *La Virgen de Guadalupe* appeared before Juan Diego, requesting that a church be built in her honor in Tepeyac. The Virgin asked Juan Diego to communicate her desire to the bishop, who did not believe him. Finally, the Virgin granted Juan Diego a sign; she gave him roses that do not flower in the hills of Tepeyac. When

Juan Diego returned to the bishop, he carried not only the roses, but also the semblance of the Virgin on his blanket. With these signs, Juan Diego was able to convince the bishop to build a church in her honor. Cisneros places her story at the heart of the religious Mexican culture, both ancient and modern. Today, Tepeyac is a popular tourist attraction, where people can buy photographs of themselves placed against the backdrop of an historical canvas. In this religious town, where everyone except the narrator's grandfather believes in the legend of Juan Diego, the narrator captures the past, the present, and the future of the town and of her grandfather.

The Mexican culture worships *La Virgen de Guadalupe,* "the first dark Mestiza Virgin" (Rebolledo 50). In another of Cisneros's stories, "Little Miracles, Kept Promises," the character Chayo adopts this mythological rendition of *La Virgen* to empower herself and to discard the Virgin who is traditionally passive and unselfish. Instead, Chayo refers to la Virgen's long history of uniting the people to fight for their rights, like the César Chavez farm workers' strike.

"Tepeyac" is not only significant because of its historical backdrop, but also because it becomes part of a literary manifesto when the narrator reveals that she will remember and record the past. The story begins with the narrator's memory of meeting her grandfather at his *tlapalería* shop and walking him home. They begin their walk home toward La Fortuna, number 12, the place "that has always been our house" (*Woman Hollering* 22–23). As they climb the twenty-two steps to the house, the narrator's focus shifts back and forth, between past and present. It begins in the past, with the memories of the narrator's routine with her grandfather: At sixteen, seventeen, and eighteen years of age, the narrator shifts to the time when the grandchild leaves and loses contact with her grandfather. The narrator keeps counting the changes in the past, up to the point when La Fortuna was sold, and on to when the *tlapalería* changes owners, and to when her grandfather dies. She is then in the present, at number *veintisiete* (twenty-seven), a number beyond the steps. Twenty-seven suggests the age of the narrator as she returns to her grandparents' home. For each step going forward, the narrator returns to her memories of the past, which are so much more than the static photographs or souvenirs of Tepeyac or *La Virgen.* Her memories hold the very essence of her past, the unnamable, her grandfather's story, her grandfather's memory. The narrator and her memories stand in stark contrast to the commercialized souvenirs of *Recuerdo de Tepeyac*—backdrops against which tourists can insert themselves—and the souvenirs of *La Virgen,* where one can buy history on a little card. The narrator will write about what she remembers of Tepeyac and that "something irretrievable" that has been buried with her grandfather. The Mexican past that the child shared with her grandfather is unrecoverable, and so is the end of childhood in the first part of the collection. Like many Mexicans, this grandchild left and returned, years later, from "that borrowed country" (23) (like the "barbaric country" of the previous story). The town she returns to is decrepit, and the small-town life that she remembers has disappeared; it has given way to modernization, to automobiles, and to diesel fumes.

Part II, "One Holy Night," contains only two stories about adolescence and the inherent dangers of sexual love. The narrators are both young adolescent girls on the brink of womanhood who learn through dangerous circumstances what it means to participate in sexual love. If the tone of Part I was mostly about family security, the two stories that make up the second part portray a sense of danger and the darker side of love. They examine the risks inherent in teenage sex, like pregnancy, rape, abuse, kidnapping, and even murder. As young girls become young women, they also become sexual objects, and they face the risk of being abused by men. As the focus of the child Latina shifts from imaginary play and female best friends to the opposite sex, Cisneros portrays the undercurrent of potential dangers and violence that accompany maturation and loss of innocence.

"One Holy Night," the title story of the section, stands out because of its engagement with ancient Mayan legends. The story is told retrospectively from the point of view of a thirteen-year-old who is now in Mexico because she is pregnant. The narrator tells the reader of her "one holy night" with Chaq Uxmal Paloquín, who turns out to be a forty-year-old serial killer who has murdered eleven girls. Boy Baby, the English translation of *nene niño*, seduces the narrator by creating a world of Mayan myths. He claims he is from an ancient line of Mayan kings and, after raping her, names her Ixchel, his queen.

The narrator who, at the time, lived with her grandmother and her Uncle Lalo, regularly helped her uncle with his pushcart, selling mango sticks and cucumbers spears across the border, in the United States. One day, Boy Baby or Chaq Uxmal Paloquín, bought food from her and eventually took her to his room, where he seduced her. He tells her that he comes from an ancient line of Mayan kings from the Yucatán, "Chaq of the people of the sun, Chaq of the temples" (*Woman Hollering* 29). As she is being violated, the narrator remembers the ancient Mayan kingdoms. For the narrator, this initiation into womanhood, despite the potential violence that might have accompanied it, is a moment to celebrate. She declares that she has become a part of female history, of womanhood. The narrator does not feel that the sexual act is something to be ashamed of, but rather something to celebrate. In the end, despite the dangerous circumstances facing the narrator, the narrator remembers her "rape" as an initiation into a long history of womanhood, of ancient myths and traditions, as a beautiful experience of love, as "one holy night." She actually admits to loving Boy Baby, and she decides to name her child *Alegre* (Happy) because there is such misery in the world and because "life will always be hard" (35).

Aside from the Mayan lore, the story's more gritty theme is the cycle of teenage pregnancy. This young teenage girl will become a mother without a husband, just as her mother was. The narrator's grandmother and Uncle Lalo send her to the other side of the border, to San Dionisio de Tlaltepango in Mexico, to have the baby. The *abuelita* blames Uncle Lalo for his goddaughter's pregnancy. But, the narrator notes that Mexico is where she was conceived illegitimately when her own mother became pregnant at a young age. The cycle of illegitimate children is continued throughout the female line, "My mother took the crooked walk too, I'm told, and I'm sure my Abuelita has her own story" (*Woman Hollering* 28).

Part III is Cisneros's most accomplished section with respect to the incorporation of cultural elements and contemporary North American society. The thirteen stories that make up "There Was a Man, There Was a Woman," deal with gender issues, as the title reflects, but gender issues rooted in a traditional patriarchal Mexican society and confronted with new-found customs and traditions that characterize the United States. With the exception of "Eyes of Zapata," all of the stories are set within contemporary society. Three stories form the crux of this section: "Woman Hollering Creek," "Eyes of Zapata," and "*Bien* Pretty." Each of these are almost double the length of the five intervening stories and, taken together, they reveal both contemporary and historic issues challenging Mexican/Chicana/Latina women. In each of these stories the woman is empowering herself slowly. "*Bien* Pretty," which ends the collection, is about Lupe, who is finally able to discard the role imposed on her by the traditional, patriarchal Mexican system, and who is ready to live alone, to be empowered and liberated.

In the stories "Woman Hollering Creek," "Eyes of Zapata," and "*Bien* Pretty," Cisneros pays homage to and plays with Mexican national history and myths. *La Llorona*, the Mexican Revolution, and the ancient Aztec volcano myth of *el Príncipe Popocatépetl*, and *la Princesa Ixtaccíhuatl* are twisted and reinvented into new images. In "Woman Hollering Creek" *La Llorona* becomes la Gritona. In "Eyes of Zapata," Zapata's lover is the main character, while the heroic figure Zapata is asleep throughout the story. In "*Bien* Pretty," the myth of the prince and princess is revisualized and repainted, this time with the princess standing over the dead prince, and not vice versa.

La Llorona, the wailing woman, is the legend that appears in the title story "Woman Hollering Creek." It is not certain when the image of *La Llorona* was born, but it is clear that the image of *La Llorona* has merged with that of La Malinche, the Nahuatl princess of the sixteenth century. In this sense, the legend brings together Indian and Spanish folklore (Rebolledo 62). When the Spanish conquistador Hernán Cortés arrived in Mexico in 1531, he was given a noble Nahuatl princess called Marina, or La Malinche. La Malinche, able to speak Quiche and Nahuatl, quickly learned Spanish and served as translator among the many tribes in Mexico, thus aiding Cortés in the conquest of Mexico. Because she helped Cortés, she has historically been viewed as a traitor to Mexico. According to Rudolfo Anaya, who writes his own version of the legend in *The Legend of La Llorona,* La Malinche realizes that the Spanish conquest will not lead to a new harmonious and better life for her people. In shame and despair, anger and pain, she sacrifices her two sons. La Malinche becomes *La Llorona.* There are hundreds of versions of the legend, but the central tenet is always the same: a woman drowns her children in the river because her husband or lover has left her, will not marry her, or will not take her children. Her spirit wanders the river, looking for the children she has drowned. In effect, "The image is a negative one, tied up in some vague way with sexuality and the death or loss of children: the negative mother image" (Rebolledo 63). In "Woman Hollering Creek," Cisneros plays with this legend, revisiting and reinventing the tragic ending.

The story begins with the marriage of Cleófilas to Juan Pedro Martínez Sánchez. Cleófilas is given away by her father, as a possession, to Juan Pedro. At the same time, however, Cisneros describes the father in a kindly manner. He says to Cleófilas: "I am your father, I will never abandon you" (*Woman Hollering* 43). Because his job is *en el otro lado* (on the other side of the border), Cleófilas moves with Juan Pedro to Seguín, Texas. When she first crosses the little *arroyo* (creek) that divides Mexico from Texas, she wonders and laughs at the name of the creek, *La Gritona* (Woman Hollering): "Such a funny name for a creek so pretty and full of happily ever after" (*Woman Hollering* 47). She hopes that her new life as a married woman will also be a happily ever after life, like those she has seen in the *telenovela* (soap operas), with names like *Tú o Nadie* (*You or No One),* whose main message is that to love is to suffer and that to suffer for love "is good. The pain all sweet somehow. In the end" (*Woman Hollering* 45). Cleófilas discovers that to live in this illusion is difficult and, finally, impossible. From the moment she arrives in Seguín, ready to be a good housewife and mother, to make a nice home full of love, she is abused by Juan Pedro. Instead of the love she imagines will come her way, as in the soap operas or in her precious Corín Tellado romance novels, it becomes clear that her life in Seguín will be both uneventful and violent. Juan Pedro beats her periodically, leaves her isolated, and cheats on her. The more isolated and lonely she becomes, the more Cleófilas fixates on the creek. Her fascination leads her to ask her neighbors about the origin of the name. Soledad and Dolores, whose names mean "solitude" and "pain," do not remember why the little creek is called *La Gritona* (Woman Hollering). As Cleófilas endures her marriage, the suffering and the loneliness, she wonders if the real name of the creek is *La Llorona.*

As Cleófilas becomes convinced that the creek is *La Llorona,* she becomes more depressed. However, instead of submitting to the story of the legend, Cleófilas seeks help and finds it in two women named Felice and Graciela, "Happiness" and "Grace." When she goes to the doctor, she conveys her troubles to Graciela, who describes her as "bride from across the border," abused by her husband. With the help of Felice, Graciela helps arrange

Cleófilas's escape. Felice drives Cleófilas across the border and back to her home. As they cross the border, Felice, a woman with her own pickup, lets out a Tarzan yell that first amazes Cleófilas and then causes her to laugh. It is not a laughter hoping for a happy ever after life, but a laughter of recognition and, perhaps, of impending freedom. At the end of the story, Cleófilas tells the story, not of her abuse or her shame, but of this amazing woman, who "was like no woman she'd ever met" (*Woman Hollering* 56). Cleófilas is empowered enough to tell the story and to remember the "mariachi yell" of the woman hollering, the new symbol of the creek. She also remembers her own laughter, and the story closes with laughter and with water, symbols of a new life. Cleófilas, who at the beginning of the story is a traditional Mexican woman from the other side of the border, living in a world of soap operas and agreeing to be "given" in marriage to a man she does not know, becomes empowered. By the end of the story, Cleófilas realizes that she cannot remain a traditional Mexican daughter because it leads to abuse. She has new role models, Felice and Graciela. Although we don't know how Cleófilas will incorporate her pivotal experience of Seguín, Texas, now that she is back on the other side of the border, we know she has achieved awareness.

"Eyes of Zapata,"[1] at the center of Part III, is the only story in the collection that takes place in the past. "Eyes of Zapata" revisits the most important event in Mexican history, the Mexican Revolution. The Mexican Revolution, which took place from 1910–1920, was a revolution of agrarian and social reform. It was the first revolution to involve the masses: *mestizos* (mixed races), *indios* (Indians), *mexicanos pobres* (poor Mexicans), and *campesinos* (farm laborers). The goal of the revolution was the redistribution of land, taking land away from the wealthy and giving land to the poor. Emiliano Zapata, along with Pancho Villa, was one of the main heroes of the revolution; he led the revolution from southern Mexico on the side of the *campesinos*. Zapata's main slogan was "Tierra y Libertad" ("Land and Liberty"), and *la Virgen de Guadalupe* was his protector. The revolution lives on in Mexico's collective memory, both historically and fictionally. The Zapatista rebellion, *Ejército Zapatista*, which began in 1992 in the southern state of Chiapas, is an example of the recent struggle between the *indios* and the government over land rights. In writing about the revolution, Cisneros consciously places herself alongside a host of typically male Mexican writers who have revisited the event, beginning with Mariano Azuela's novel *Los de abajo*, written in 1915. Although her title, "Eyes of Zapata," alludes to the hero, the story is told exclusively from the point of view of Inés Alfaro, one of Zapata's many lovers. Zapata remains asleep during the whole narration, allowing Inés to tell the story from her point of view and without any objections or interruptions from the man. Inés is active; Zapata is passive. Cisneros plays with Mexican national history by giving voice to the women who were part of this canonical event. It was, in fact, a time when women adopted new roles and participated in the revolution either as *soldaderas* or *adelitas,* women who followed the men, not only preparing meals for them but, oftentimes, fighting alongside them (Rebolledo, Chapter 3).

Aside from the historical rendition of the revolution, "Eyes of Zapata" is a love story. Inés, as she gazes at Zapata's sleeping body, describes how they met and fell in love and how their love grew. Though Zapata became a hero, he was still a man when he visited her. As she narrates their story, she also describes her familial history as the daughter of a *bruja* (witch) from whom she inherited her powers. Inés, for example, is able to leave her earthly body but is also able to see the horror of the future and the sell-out of the Mexican Revolution. Inés has power, but this power works against her since she poses a threat to gender relations. Her mother, who also possessed these powers, was ostracized and then killed. In fact, the narration actually takes place when Inés's spirit soars above her body, traveling through time, to review the past, present, and future. She sees that Zapata has failed and is betrayed and assassinated in 1919 by one of his own. In turn, the revolution has failed; politicians and the Institutional Revolutionary Party have failed to uphold the radical and new constitution of 1917. Finally, on a personal note, Zapata has failed Inés. The question remains linked to the revolution, for how can a revolution win if gender relations still fail, if the war in the bedroom remains? The personal, then, becomes a parallel for the political. Inés's failed love for Zapata, who never marries her and is never faithful to her, serves as a parallel to the failed revolution. Again, woman is central to the revision of the past. Cisneros emphasizes that gender relations are at the center of history and of all historical events. The one that takes place in private is just as revolutionary and heroic as the one that takes place on the battlefield.

Inés understands the problem, the core of the difficulties between man and woman. Although the Mexican Revolution was an attempt to build a new national identity, women were left behind. It is not until we reach the contemporary new age of the Latina, Chicana woman that we see a reconciliation of the problems of love, gender, identity, and self. "Eyes of Zapata" stands at the center of Part III because it links past and present gender issues, demonstrating that aside from "dragging our bodies around," as Inés says, the Mexican woman has "dragged" around the same gender issues for centuries. Inés's observations and conclusions are, in many ways, the same ones that Lupe Arredondo will reach in the final story of the collection "*Bien* Pretty." In fact, the three central stories of Part III portray a woman who has achieved a final liberation and resolution of her self. "*Bien* Pretty" takes place in contemporary San Antonio, Texas, where the author Cisneros currently lives. However, Cisneros again returns to a traditional Aztec legend, that of *el Príncipe Popo* and the *Princesa Ixta,* a kind of Romeo and Juliet story. According to the legend, the Prince is drawn away to war, as was typical during the time of the Aztec empire and their warring states and tribes. While he is away, his enemies tell the princess that her lover has been killed in battle. The princess kills herself. When the prince finds out he creates two volcanoes, which stand outside of Mexico City. In one he buries his lover, and at the other he stands guard over his princess. Cisneros will play with this just as she did with *La Llorona* and with Zapata.

In many respects, San Antonio is the heart of Mexico in the United States. Texas is the state of the Alamo and like Lupe's mother says, Mexico lost all of its northern land because of a "Teja-NO-te for *tejano*, which is sort of like 'Texessive,' in a redneck kind of way" (*Woman Hollering* 142). Lupe's mother is critical of Texas's role in the Mexican American War of 1846–48. Lupe Arredondo, a San Franciscan Chicana artist, who participated in the first César Chavez grape strikes, is moving to San Antonio for no good reason except that she's been dumped by her boyfriend Eddie.

In San Antonio, she meets Flavio Mungía, a Mexican from Michoacán who has found work as a cockroach exterminator. Lupe is immediately attracted to Flavio just as she is attracted to the New Age movement, Ying and Yang, rose-quartz crystals, Tibetan gongs, Aztec ocarinas, the I Ching, the Tao, and the Popol Vuh. She characterizes her lover's face as that of an Olmec (ancient Mexican heads carved in stone), like a face an archeologist might "unearth in Teotihuacán," like a Tarascan face, "something that ought to be set in jade" (154). She decides that he will model for her as her Prince Popo in her next painting. She asks Flavio to be her model, and she falls in love with him. She wants to be in love with what looks like an authentic Mexican with Indian blood, with a past, with roots that might become hers. In fact, Lupe wants cultural artifacts and cultural fads to fill her search, to tell her who she is. She wants Flavio to fill her Mexicanness and to supply a ready-made identity that she can adopt. But, Flavio balks at this job. Flavio does not want this job, nor does he like feeling as if he is simply another cultural artifact, like her grandmother's *molcajete* (mortar). The final blow to Lupe comes when she criticizes Flavio's clothes, his Reeboks and Izod shirt. Flavio responds that he does not need to wear a *serape* (shawl) and a sombrero to know he is Mexican. He tells her that she is not Mexican. This is what Lupe fears most because she has embraced her Mexican heritage; she was one of the first to join the César Chávez grape strikes. But, she is not Mexican the way Flavio is, and she never will be. As she tells the reader, she is a product of her American education.

Despite the fact that Flavio leaves Lupe because he has wives and children on the other side of the border, this traditional macho Mexican is the first person to make her realize that her search is focused on the wrong things. When Flavio leaves Lupe, to return to his seven sons by two different wives back in Mexico, she grieves, watches *telenovelas*, and has several realizations that lead to her final awareness: "Me and me." However, Lupe has many small realizations: she wants to emulate the strong women who raised her, not those on the *telenovelas;* she has always been in love with a man; "*Life is an absurd wound*" but not something to die for; Flavio's poetry was actually pretty corny; "Our mamas and *tías.* Passionate *and* powerful, tender and volatile, brave. And, above all, fierce" (*Woman Hollering* 161). Lupe's final realization is that she, and all women, need to live: "We're going to right the world and live. I mean live our lives the way lives were meant to be lived. With the throat and wrists. With rage and desire, and joy and grief, and love till it hurts, maybe. But godamn, girl. Live" (*Woman Hollering* 163). With this realization, Lupe returns to her painting, but she alters the gender roles. Her Prince Popo is asleep (just as Zapata is asleep), and the princess is standing over him. The story of Lupe Arredondo ends the collection because, of all of the women in the twenty-two stories, she is the one who finally finds form for her identity and the right time period in which to carry out her new vision.

NOTE

1. Cisneros relied heavily on John Womack's biography of Zapata to re-create pivotal events of his life. In Womack's biography, however, Inés is merely a footnote; in Cisneros's story, she is the protagonist.

FURTHER SUGGESTED READINGS

Works by Sandra Cisnernos

Cisneros, Sandra. *Caramelo.* New York: Knopf, 2002.
———. *Loose Woman: Poems.* New York: Knopf, 1994.
———. *My Wicked Wicked Ways.* New York: Random House, 1992.
———. *Woman Hollering Creek and Other Stories.* New York: Random House, 1991.
———. *The House on Mango Street.* Houston: Arte Público Press, 1984.

Other Suggested Readings

Anaya, Rudolfo. *Maya's Children: The Story of La Llorona.* New York: Hyperion Books, 1997.
Azuela, Mariano. *Los de Abajo.* New York: Penguin Books, 1997.
Calderón, Héctor. " 'Como Mexico No Hay Dos': Sandra Cisneros's Feminist Border Stories." *Narratives of Greater Mexico: Essays on Chicano Literary History, Genre and Borders.* Austin: University of Texas Press (forthcoming).
Castillo, Ana. *So Far from God.* New York: Plume, 1994.
Chávez, Denise. *Loving Pedro Infante.* New York: Farrar, Straus & Giroux, 2000.
———. *Face of an Angel.* New York: Farrar, Straus & Giroux, 1994.
———. *The Last of the Menu Girls.* Houston: Arte Público Press, 1986.
Lewis, L.M. "Ethnic and Gender Identity: Parallel Growth in Sandra Cisneros' *Woman Hollering Creek.*" *Short Story* 2:2 (1994): 69–78.

Moraga, Cherríe, Alma Gómez, and Mariana Romo-Carmona. *Cuentos: Stories by Latinas.* New York: Kitchen Table Press; Women of Color Press, 1983.

Moraga, Cherrie and Gloria Anzaldùa, eds. *This Bridge Called My Back: Writings by Radical Women of Color.* New York: Kitchen Table Press; Women of Color Press, 1981.

Payant, Katherine. "Borderland Themes in Sandra Cisneros's *Woman Hollering Creek.*" *The Immigrant Experience in North American Literature: Carving Out a Niche.* Ed. Katherine Payant and Toby Rose. Westport and London: Greenwood Press, 1999. 95–109.

Pineda, Cecilia. *Fishlight: A Novel of Childhood.* San Antonio: Wings Press, 2001.

Viramontes, Helena María. *Under the Feet of Jesus.* New York: Dutton/Plume, 1995.

———. *The Moths and Other Stories.* Houston, Arte Público Press, 1985.

Womack, John. *Zapata and the Mexican Revolution.* New York: Random House, 1970.

Chapter 4
The Fiction of Junot Díaz: Drown (1996)

J unot Díaz is one of the few male Dominican writers writing in English today. He was born in the Dominican Republic in 1968 and moved to New Jersey with his family when he was six years old. After attending public schools in New Jersey, Díaz graduated from Rutgers University and went on to receive his M.F.A in writing from Cornell University. Describing himself as "the one who left and never really came back" (Rocco 3) to his community except through the written word, Díaz began writing *por casualidad* (by chance). Soon, however, he became committed to conveying "on paper" his experiences of the life he left behind on the island, and his life as a child in a *barrio* on the mainland (*New York Times Talk Series*). Díaz has always felt a profound obligation to write "to [his] community, not about it" (Rocco 3). His acknowledgements in *Drown* illustrate his commitment; he recognizes, "A debt to the community, especially Barrio XXI. And to those who watch over us."

Díaz's stories have been published in *The New Yorker, The Paris Review,* and *African Voices*. Six of the stories already published, and four new stories, became *Drown*, published in 1996 to wide critical acclaim. Díaz was named one of *Newsweek*'s "New Faces of 1996." Since the publication of *Drown*, Diaz has continued to publish stories in *The New Yorker*. One story that stands out is, "The Brief Wondrous Life of Oscar Wao." In this black comedy, Díaz explores the life of Oscar de León, a Dominican boy who never quite becomes the traditional macho male. In addition, instead of the tale of an immigrant family moving north, from the island to the mainland, it portrays an established Dominican family in the 1970s, just as

Oscar is headed to the Dominican Republic. Currently, Díaz teaches English at Syracuse University in New York. He is finishing work on his first novel.

Drown is modeled after Díaz's own family and their experiences as immigrants in New Jersey. Díaz dedicates the collection to his mother, who said of the collection: "This is so much about us, yet it has nothing to do with us" (Zeledón 2). In the collection, Díaz explores the complexities of the Dominican community and the immigrant experience. His novel moves between Santo Domingo and the urban setting of Washington Heights, New Jersey. Díaz illustrates how the sacrifices of immigration damage the family. The reviewer Claudia Rocco notes, "These pressures and sacrifices figure prominently in his writing, which explores the intimate world of families and lovers in the Dominican Republic and urban America. His characters struggle with poverty, with absent fathers, with inner worlds and longings at odds with outer realities and expectations" (2).

Aside from the personal meditation on the ravages of immigration, Díaz wants to make a political statement. Of all of the writers included here, Díaz is the most radical and the most critical of the role the United States has played in creating a gap between "the world that they [politicians and government] swear exists and the world that I know exists [that of immigrants, poverty, African Americans, inner cities]" (*The Beacon Best of 2001* 3). A gap exists between what Diaz calls the "real story," the life that he experienced as a child and that he witnesses now as an activist, and the "official story," that all is well and is growing. According to Díaz, the "real story" is displaced by the distortions, silences, and erasures perpetrated by the media, politicians, and public schools. For Díaz, *Drown* fills in the gap, portraying the hardships of urban immigrants, while also accusing institutions like public schools, as do Cisneros and Quiñonez.

The title *Drown* symbolizes the inherent risks of immigration. Immigrants may drown in the sea of American mainstream institutions; their culture may drown in the process of assimilation and, as already noted, the family may become permanently damaged by the pressures of immigration. When *Drown* was translated into Spanish, the collection was renamed *Negocios,* which can mean both businesses and negotiations. *Negocios* also maintains a symbolic meaning since it represents the imposing daily task of negotiating not only between two cultures, but also between family and work, between old traditions and new ideas, between the dignity and compromise that accompany poverty, between racism and assimilation. Perhaps for the sake of the Spanish readers, Díaz wanted to acknowledge their daily struggle in a more positive way. For English readers, *Drown* emphasizes the more bleak idea that immigrants struggle to prevent from drowning.

The ten stories in *Drown* can be divided into two general groups: one group follows Yunior's family, from their early years in the Dominican Republic to the later years in Washington Heights, New Jersey; the other group focus on a Yunior who has grown up and who seems a disembodied soul, whose father has already left, and whose mother is barely surviving. This Yunior deals in petty drugs, delivers pool tables, and is basically going nowhere. He is the antithesis of many of the protagonists in the novels included here (with the exception, perhaps, of the Castillo brothers in Hijuelos's novel) who end their stories on a celebratory note or return to a community in order to move ahead. The collection stands out in the sense that there is no final celebration, nor any great insight for the protagonist. In this sense, Díaz remains true to his political belief that things are not well in the inner cities and that he will not portray them as such.

Despite the discouraging tone of the collection, the reader understands that the character will survive, that he has gained the tools to carry on. This is evident in the last story, "Negocios," in which Yunior goes in search of his father's mistress Nilda, with whom the father has had two children, and attempts to piece together and understand his father's abandonment of and lack of contact with his first family. This final story reflects a more mature Yunior trying to come to terms with his past. Yunior's reconstruction of his father's years in the United States without the rest of the family is perhaps the manifestation of the future writer Díaz. With the exception of "Face," all of the stories are narrated in the first person singular by an anonymous narrator who, we assume, is Yunior. The stories are connected in that they share family details mentioned by the narrator and reveal a progression in the life of the narrator. The narrator's tone contains both nostalgia and awareness, as he examines his past life from a distance and comments on the mistakes of his youth, his innocence, and his failures. The greatest mistake of his life was to interpret his father's abuse as love. The childhood desire of the narrator, as he looks back, was the love of his father: "I still wanted him to love me, something that never seemed strange or contradictory until years later, when he was out of our lives" (*Drown* 27).

DROWN (1996)

Nine of the ten stories in *Drown* are narrated in the first person singular by Yunior, the youngest son of the de las Casas family. Five of the ten stories focus on the de las Casas family: Mami, or Virta (Virtudes); Papi, or Ramón; and their two sons, Rafa and Yunior. The five stories, "Ysrael," "Fiesta, 1980" (Party), "Aguantando" (Enduring, Surviving, Holding-on), "Drown" and "Negocios" (Businesses), fluctuate between the Dominican Republic and New Jersey and also between the abandonment and return of the father, Ramón de las Casas. In "Ysrael" and "Aguantando," Yunior is nine years old. In "Fiesta, 1980," he is older, perhaps twelve. "Negocios," narrated by the adult Yunior, depicts his father's experiences in Miami and New York. "Drown," the title story, which stands at the center of the collection, maintains ties to both categories, the family stories and the New Jersey stories.

The second group of stories, which take place in New Jersey, are: "Aurora," "Drown," "Boyfriend," "Edison, New Jersey," and "How to Date a Browngirl. . . . " These stories focus on Yunior's young-adult life in high school and during the first years after high school. "No Face" stands alone in the collection. The only story narrated in the third person singular, it returns to the character Ysrael and functions as a detailed character portrayal. The story stands as an interior running monologue in which Ysrael pretends he is a superhero and, at the same time, gives us the background information about his deformed face and his present circumstances. (It is conceivable that Yunior narrates this story, inventing what life must be like for Ysrael, especially given the empathy and concern Yunior expresses for Ysrael when they finally meet.) The story, although seemingly separate from the whole collection, shares a central theme—the absent, uncaring, and abusive father, the father who rejects the son. In this sense, it is intimately tied to what haunts Yunior throughout the collection, the relationship between himself and his father.

THE FAMILY STORIES

"Ysrael," which takes place in the Dominican Republic, introduces the reader to Yunior and Rafa, aged nine and twelve, who spend their summers in the *campo* (country) while their mother works in a chocolate factory in the city. We learn that their father has been in New York for six years and that this arouses mixed feelings in the two boys. Although in the summer Yunior is close to his brother, back in the city, in Santo Domingo, they do not get along. In this other environment, Rafa behaves like a bully and a young macho. Yunior, on the other hand, is much more innocent, sensitive, and impressionable. The plot of the story unfolds around the brothers' desire to unmask Ysrael, whose face was half-eaten by a pig when he was a baby. Ysrael's face is the topic of town rumors, "He was something to talk about, a name that set the kids to screaming, worse than el Cuco [the boogeyman] or la Vieja Calusa" (*Drown* 7).

When they finally meet, Yunior and Ysrael (both names start with "Y," as if these characters mirror each other) connect immediately. Both of their fathers are in New York, both enjoy wrestling and, as they converse, Yunior realizes that he has made Ysrael smile. In the story "No Face," which comes later in the collection, we learn this is a lie. We discover that Ysrael must leave his home every morning before his father sees him and cannot return until night. The fact remains, however, that both are abandoned by their fathers. They might have been friends if Rafa had not pursued the goal of unmasking the boy. Rafa knocks Ysrael out, and they unmask him. When they finally are able to expose Ysrael's face, the brothers are left painfully dissatisfied for different reasons. Yunior, who connects with Ysrael, understands the horror of what they have done. Rafa realizes that the promise that keeps Ysrael going—that North American doctors are going to operate on him and fix his face—is a false promise that resembles the false promises of his father's return. The story ends up being less about Ysrael and more about Yunior. Yunior knows intuitively "how easily distances could harden and become permanent" (*Drown* 75).

Aside from the story of the three boys, "Ysrael" gives a brief picture of the homeland, providing readers with a sense of the Dominican Republic and especially of the country area outside of Santo Domingo, the capital. The story is full of linguistic and cultural markers. "No Face," which functions as the other half to "Ysrael," exposing the inner thoughts of the boy under the mask, also highlights life in *el campo* (the countryside). Díaz does not italicize his Spanish, but the reader will recognize many words: *colmado* (grocery store), *ponchera* (hole puncher), *cobrador* (collector), *tío* (uncle), *campo*, and slang like *tígueres* (hooligans), *pinga* (vulgar slang for male genitalia), *chocha* (vulgar slang for female genitalia) and more. In addition to the linguistic markers, we find ourselves in the rural *campo*, where Rafa and Yunior live with their *tío* in a wooden house without electricity or television, and where cock fighting is still a major pastime.

"Fiesta, 1980" takes place in New Jersey. The family has been in the United States for three years. The story describes Yunior and his family visiting their *tía* and *tío*, the newly arrived members of the family, for a big party. Spanish is spoken by Yunior's family, except when Rafa wants to tell Yunior something in secret. The story, although about a family party, is actually about the father, Ramón de las Casas, who is not only abusive toward his children, especially Yunior, but who also has a mistress and is in the process of leaving the family. Yunior tells about how he met his father's mistress, "the Puerto Rican woman." While his father is upstairs with the mistress, Yunior sits in the living room, "ashamed, expecting something big and fiery to crash down on our heads" (*Drown* 36). The reader discovers that the father takes the boys to the Puerto Rican woman's house frequently: "The affair was like a hole in our living room floor, one we'd gotten so used to circumnavigating that we sometimes forgot it was there" (*Drown* 39–40). As in "Ysrael," the story ends with Yunior's insight and awareness of the family dynamic and struggle. This time Yunior's awareness is that his family will not remain intact.

"Aguantando," a story of waiting, returns to the Dominican Republic and, thus, takes place before 1980. Here Yunior tells us, "I lived without a father for the first nine years of my life. He was in the States, working, and the only way I knew him was through the photographs my moms kept in a plastic sandwich bag under her bed" (*Drown* 69). This story describes in detail the struggle the mother faces while the father is away. Once again, the subtext alludes to the father and the children's hope and belief that their father's return is imminent. Coupled with that anticipation is the older narrator's realization that it was hopeless: "I didn't know him at all. I didn't know that he'd abandoned us. That this waiting for him was all a sham" (*Drown* 70). The poverty, the worms, and the ostracism that the boys experience at school because they can't afford uniforms or books, are all bearable compared to hoping for their father's return. Yunior clings to this hope, despite his mother and Rafa's experience, both of whom are disillusioned. Yunior, only nine, still believes.

"Negocios," which takes place first in *la Capital*, Santo Domingo, and then in Miami and New York, ends the collection. Chronologically, it stands as the first story of the collection since it narrates the painful event of the father's departure when Yunior is four that haunts the entire collection. The story depicts Ramón de las Casas's departure to the United States and his belief in a better life there. He tells his father-in-law: "All I want for your daughter and our children is to take them to the United States. I want a good life for them" (*Drown* 164). He then borrows money from his father-in-law and uses it to disappear for the next five years with barely a word. In this story, the narrator, Yunior, is now an informed adult narrator reconstructing his father's trip. He has secured information from both his mother and father, and from his father's mistress Nilda (with whom the father also had children), to recreate the five years. His father and mother provide different versions of these years. The narrator, to supplement the story, also seeks out Nilda and records his brief encounter with her. In this regard, the story stands as a recovery story, in that Yunior, now an adult, searches and pursues sources to build his father's absent years. Yunior is a sympathetic narrator: "Don't get me wrong: it wasn't that he [Yunior's father] was having fun. No, he'd been robbed twice already, his ribs beaten until they were bruised. He often drank too much and went home to his room, and then he'd fume, spinning, angry at the stupidity that had brought him to this freezing hell of a country" (*Drown* 179). He now seeks to understand but not forgive his father. In the end, Yunior realizes that he shares something with Nilda; Ramón abandoned both of them.

The "New Jersey stories," as critic Lizabeth Paravisini-Gebert named the five stories that take place in New Jersey, describe an older Yunior, and are rooted in the urban *barrio* experience of immigrant generations. The first story, "Aurora," is both a love story gone wrong and a drug story. The characters find old, abandoned buildings, cellars, or basements in which to do drugs and create pseudo-homes. The descriptions of the drug scenes are interspersed with those of the narrator and Aurora, who is not yet seventeen years old. The last scene of the story reveals Aurora's desire to create a home, despite her addiction to drugs. Yunior reacts violently to her desire to make a home—to her romantic and perhaps hopeless dreams—by hitting her.

"Drown," the title story of the collection, and the center story, is not only a New Jersey story but also a family story. Yunior narrates the story of his relationship to Beto, as well as the broken relationship of his mother and his father. Yunior, now living with his mother (his father having left to live with another woman in Florida), remains in his limbo years, neither here nor there, undecided about his future. He describes himself: "I wasn't asleep or awake, but caught somewhere in between, rocked slowly back and forth the way surf holds junk against the shore, rolling it over and over" (*Drown* 105). The story narrates the homosexual encounters between the narrator and his best friend Beto. Beto has now graduated from high school, is in college, and is a self-declared homosexual or *pato,* the derogatory word for homosexual in much of Latin America. Yunior describes the last summer the two spend together as one when they "stole, broke windows . . . pissed on people's steps and then challenged them to come out and stop us" (*Drown* 91). Beto despises the neighborhood and is ready to leave for college. The narrator still has a year of high school left. Their last summer together shifts to a brief homosexual encounter that destroys the friendship. The narrator is not gay but allows one moment to transpire. In the end, he does not forgive Beto's transgression, though he still yearns for his friendship. This emotional turmoil mirrors that between himself, his father, and his mother. Yunior does not forgive his father for disappearing, yet he yearns for a relationship with his father. His mother feels the same way. In the end, the two, mother and son, realize that they must make a new family; it will be a family composed of the two of them, living in an apartment with the windows locked to those who bring them destruction, to those who destroy their sense of *familia* and self.

"Boyfriend," "Edison, New Jersey," and "How to Date a Browngirl, Blackgirl, Whitegirl, or Halfie," address the racial divide both in and outside the narrator's neighborhood. Manifest in each of these stories is the culture of color that characterizes and preoccupies members of the neighborhood. These stories are also meant to complicate concepts of Latino identity. In addition, they serve as a kind of slap in the face to the *mestizaje* (racial mixing) story, in which the dreaded "race mixing" is part of the culture, and in which single men need tips on how to negotiate girls of mixed color. Each of these three stories describes the understood color code that characterizes racially mixed neighborhoods. In "Boyfriend," the narrator eavesdrops on his downstairs neighbors, who are Spanish-speaking black Latinos. The breakup of the downstairs couple parallels Yunior's own recent breakup with his girlfriend Loretta. The narrator's girlfriend and the boyfriend downstairs have both broken off their relationships in order to pursue a relationship with a white person. In the narrator's opinion, the boyfriend has crossed an unspoken, yet understood, racial boundary of loyalty. Dating white girls is seen as a betrayal of the race, although the narrator himself will admit in "How to Date a Browngirl . . . " that he really wants to date white girls.

Dating a white girl is seen as a sign of success. (Hijuelos's character, Cesar Castillo, knows he has succeeded when he seduces Vanna Vane. This racial flaunting is twisted in Cisneros's story "*Bien* Pretty"; the narrator feels she has succeeded when she snares a Mexican.)

In "Edison, New Jersey," the narrator, now a college graduate and a pool-table delivery person, falls for the Dominican maid of a wealthy white man. If "Boyfriend" addressed the extant racial boundaries of the neighborhood, this story addresses the racial, social, and class divide that exists outside the neighborhood. The narrator delivers pool tables to the wealthy and describes their uneasiness with trusting him because he is not white. The narrator, fully aware of their unease, develops petty games in order to retaliate against the hidden racial prejudices. As in the previous story, the narrator's girlfriend has recently broken up with him and is dating a white *gringo* named Dan, who works on Wall Street. His girlfriend tells the narrator that she likes her new boyfriend because he works hard. As the narrator reflects on this, he tries to date the Dominican maid who is in love with her white boss.

Although it is a tongue-in-cheek story, an ironic and comical self-help manual, "How to Date a Browngirl, Blackgirl, Whitegirl or Halfie" illustrates the deeper issues beneath racial labeling. Instead of analyzing the forces of racism from a sociological or political perspective, the narrator comments on the hazards of dating girls of different colors, and gives instructions on how to play the game and successfully "score" with them. It is a story that celebrates hybridism. Interdating, like intermarriage, remains taboo in the Anglo dominant culture. But, in this story, it is perfectly acceptable for a young Latino man to choose to date, and to *want* to date a brown girl, a white girl, a black girl or a halfie. The narrator also reflects on the psychological underpinnings that characterize interracial dating. Depending on the girl's color, the narrator has a different tactic, as different mixes require different seductions. Halfies are insecure and apologetic, and they admit that they are not accepted by blacks, being held responsible for the black parent's racial betrayal: "Black people, she will say, treat me real bad. That's why I don't like them" (*Drown* 147). White girls are the desired ones: "You love them more than you love your own" (*Drown* 147). In retrospect, the adult narrator realizes that dating a white woman signifies turning one's back on one's race.

"No Face" and "Negocios," already discussed, end the collection, returning us to Santo Domingo and to the father's immigration to the United States. Aside from the absent father theme, both stories share the dream of emigrating to the United States for a better life. Ysrael, in "No Face," hopes for the operation he has been promised. Yunior's father hopes for a better life. Ysrael never makes it to the United States, and Yunior's father's dreams of a better life are thwarted as soon as he arrives.

CULTURAL ELEMENTS

Drown centers on the hardships stemming from immigration and poverty. Dominican culture is subsumed within the daily struggles that typify immigration, language issues, economic hardship, racism, and alienation. The ten stories, connected by the narrator and protagonist of the de las Casas family, illustrate how poverty and immigration can destroy a family. In this case, the de las Casas's difficulties are compounded by the father's old-fashioned patriarchal ways, his violent and abusive nature, and his self-righteous attitude about being unfaithful to his wife. Díaz does not focus on the issues that confront the bilingual and bicultural individual, but rather on one immigrant family on the mainland. Unlike many of the other novels analyzed here, in fact, there is no sense of community portrayed in *Drown*. That connective tissue of aunts, sisters, fortunetellers, or of community members who aid in the main protagonist's survival and self-understanding is almost completely lacking. Rather, Díaz describes a world of urban despair in which the main protagonist, Yunior, unable to understand the world, harboring hatred, and lacking self-respect is drawn to the world of drugs. Díaz seems to be saying that immigration is the root of the family's troubles.

"Negocios," more than any other story in the collection, focuses on the actual experiences and hardships of young Latino men attempting to succeed in the United States. It resembles the story of Guzmán in Judith Ortiz Cofer's *The Line of the Sun* and of Geraldo in Cisneros's story "Geraldo No Last Name." Young male Latinos who arrive in the United States seeking better economic opportunities and a better life for their families, who are, many times, left behind, struggle with racism and exploitation. They face daily negotiations and compromises in their desire to succeed. Ramón de las Casas, who leaves the Dominican Republic because of the rampant unemployment on the island, begs his father-in-law to give him the money for airfare. Like most immigrants, Ramón believes he will make his fortune in the United States and then return. However, the struggle lasts longer than expected, with one obstacle after another. Ramón is called a "spik," loses several jobs for no reason, receives no benefits or security, and is swindled by other immigrants who have been in the United States longer. With the realization that return will be impossible, the goal becomes to "get your *familia* over here and buy yourself a nice house and start branching out. That's the American way" (*Drown* 190). Initially, however, like many immigrants, Ramón is sidetracked by his dreams of fortune: "He was twenty-four. He didn't dream about his *familia* and wouldn't for many years. He dreamed instead of gold coins, like the ones that had been salvaged from the many wrecks about our island, stacked high as sugar cane" (*Drown* 169). He would not be able to bring his family over until the narrator is nine, five years after his departure from the Dominican Republic.

Ramón's journey from the Dominican Republic, his different jobs, and his difficulty securing American citizenship represents that of "most immigrants around them" (*Drown* 188). Díaz highlights the historical draw and the chronological order of the Spanish Caribbean immigrants to New York by contextualizing Ramón's journey. Ramón is one of thousands on a journey toward *Nueva Yol* (New York), "the city of jobs, the city that had first called the Cubanos and their cigar industry, then the Bootstrap Puerto Ricans and now him" (*Drown* 167). When Ramón first arrives he does not understand North American politics or culture; he even wonders if there might be a curfew, as there had been frequently on his island. Soon Ramón is impressed with the cleanliness and orderliness of the neighborhoods and streets in the United States. However, his good impressions of the United States will quickly be replaced by the many obstacles impeding his search for his fortune. The focus of life for the low-income, low-wage immigrant shifts from dreams of gold to hopes of survival.

The immigrant experience is not only an encounter between the immigrant and the United States but also between the immigrant and transplanted workers from other Latin American countries. A community of immigrants and networks exists with both good advice and bad advice. When Ramón arrives, a Spanish cab driver recognizes that he is an immigrant and remarks, "A new one," meaning yet another immigrant (*Drown* 167). When the cab driver asks about a place for Ramón or if he has family, Ramón answers ingenuously, "I got two hands and a heart as strong as a rock." The cab driver simply responds "Right," knowing that even two hands and a strong heart will not do, given the obstacles that face Ramón (*Drown* 168). The cab driver refuses payment, telling Ramón that he will need every cent for rent. He is told to find a job immediately, to learn English as quickly as he can, and to save all of his money. Everyone advises him against a job in a *fábrica* (factory). But there are other immigrants who see those recently arrived as targets to abuse, especially when it comes to paying for American citizenship. Ramón, after losing $800 in his attempt to secure citizenship through marriage, records his experience as a cautionary tale for the next immigrant who will live in his apartment.

Although there are some immigrants who become successful, like Jo-Jo and Nilda (Ramón marries Nilda in order to secure American citizenship), most become caught in a financial trap. They work twenty-hour days, seven days a week for low wages, making only enough money to pay rent and send some money home. Sometimes, as in Ramón's case, sending money home leaves him broke and forced to borrow more money. In this way, a vicious cycle evolves in which the immigrant worker is not paid enough, struggles to pay rent, loses his job or his apartment, and is set adrift once again looking for another job without benefits or security. Ramón, also like many others, decides to move to New York. He walks and hitchhikes all the way from Miami, 380 miles, saving his money for rent because, as he is told by "veteran immigrants": "To be homeless in Nueva York was to court the worst sort of disaster" (*Drown* 174). Ramón eventually becomes successful in that he learns English well enough to communicate, and he finds a stable job in New York. He also marries another Dominican, Nilda, for American citizenship without telling her of his family in Santo Domingo. This infidelity is accepted by other immigrants and is seen as a temporary step toward securing citizenship. The marriage, meant only to secure papers, is also meant to end after a couple of months. Ramón, however, moves in with Nilda and becomes accustomed to their life together. They even have a son. Ramón's friends see this as a betrayal of the necessary steps toward success in America, and they urge him to bring his first *familia* to the mainland. Loyalty to the *familia* takes precedence, and friends who learn of Ramón's family in the Dominican Republic repeatedly chastise him and tell him to bring them over.

The *familia* in the Dominican Republic, and Nilda in the United States, learn about each other's families. The wives live with this arrangement, but not quietly. Ramón's wife in the Dominican Republic sends him monthly letters scolding him and reminding him of his responsibilities. The longer Ramón lives with Nilda, however, the more entrenched he becomes. He even returns to the Dominican Republic with Nilda, where he feels like a "tourist," and does not visit his first family. Eventually, however, his life with Nilda sours, and he sees his first *familia* "as a regenerative force that could redeem his fortunes" (*Drown* 204–05). He leaves Nilda, returns to the Dominican Republic, and brings his family to the United States. The reader knows that, a couple of years later, he will abandon them as well.

Aside from the troubles of immigration, Díaz also focuses on the drug culture that flourishes in inner cities. Because there are no positive outlets or role models for the children of immigrants, they turn to drugs as a way of gaining income and of escaping their bleak future. Drugs, which transcend socioeconomic barriers, have played a big part in the lives of young male Dominicans. The Dominican riots of 1992, as they have been called, began when a drug dealer was shot to death by the police. The shooting set off riots (Winn 586) that left Washington Heights devastated, and it created another stereotype of Latinos in the United States. Puerto Ricans and Dominicans, especially the men, were portrayed by the media as drug addicts. Díaz's main character is lured into the drug culture not only because of a sense of hopelessness, but also to make money. As a peddler, the protagonist reflects on the pervasiveness of drugs, observing that drug use defies racial, economic, and social barriers. His customers are poor, rich, young, old, professional, and addicts. Although the protagonist is temporarily involved in drugs, he does not become addicted like the other characters he describes. The drug culture is also included in the work of other inner-city authors, such as Piri Thomas and Abraham Rodríguez, who link the drug culture to a lack of empowerment. Criticism is directed at the gov-

ernment at large, but much more specifically at the educators in the public
schools, and at the lack of trust and hope that they place on Latino youth
and their communities. The public school system, also seen in the work of
Quiñonez and Cisneros, offers little hope for young Latinos and cripples
their budding sense of personal and collective self-respect.

In the story "Drown," a teacher in the protagonist's school tells the students, as they watch a space shuttle launch, that many of them will not make
it, but will burn out. "Drown" offers the reader the picture of a young male
Latino headed nowhere fast. The narrator, on the verge of graduating from
high school, has no future options, unlike his friend Beto. He suggests that
he is enacting the self-fulfilling prophecy that society has of young, male
Latinos.

Gender roles follow the typical expectations for men and women in a
patriarchal system, the male macho and the submissive Latina. In the immigrant situation, the patriarchal system can have further negative effects when
husbands prevent their wives from working, frustrate their attempts to pursue educational opportunities, or even prohibit them from learning the language. Wives are not supposed to become independent in any way, as it
threatens the husband's manhood and the patriarchal order. This is vividly
portrayed in Cisneros's *The House on Mango Street,* where women are literally locked behind doors and windows, prevented from bettering themselves, expected to remain submissive, and restricted to domestic chores.
They are expected to remain quiet while their husbands cheat on them.
Yunior's mother is considered by the father to be useless, except to feed the
children and keep house. According to the narrator, all Dominican women
are seen this way. In the story "Fiesta, 1980," the women spend hours
thanklessly cooking food for the husbands and children, which is the
Dominican tradition.

Yunior's father is no exception to the cultural stereotype of machismo.
Yunior describes him as the typical violent macho, "Papi was old-fashioned;
he expected your undivided attention when you were getting your ass
whupped" (*Drown* 26). The "'Macho' is the accepted—and expected—
single-word description synonymous with Latino men and male culture"
(Rivera 502). The protagonist's father is accustomed to the idea that he can
have a mistress and have his wife there to serve him, and he should also be
allowed to react violently when things are not as he expects them to be. It
is accepted that the young males of the family prove their masculinity
through sex, the earlier the better. Rafa, Yunior's brother, at the age of
twelve, attempts to seduce as many women as possible. In "Fiesta, 1980,"
Yunior's uncle, in talking about Yunior's nine years of age, tells his mother,
"Young? Back in Santo Domingo, he'd be getting laid by now" (*Drown* 31).
In "Edison, New Jersey," when the narrator and his girlfriend are in Florida,
the girlfriend does not want the narrator's mother to see pictures of her in
a bikini because she doesn't want to be thought of as a whore (*Drown* 136).

The father is not ridiculed for his philandering, whereas the woman is always considered a *sucia* or *puta* (dirty or whore) for engaging in the same behavior.

Race for Díaz is linked to personal relationships. "Boyfriend," "Edison, New Jersey," and "How to Date a Browngirl . . . ," all have a narrator who has recently broken up with his girlfriend or who is trying to date. Love, dating, and breaking up expose racial issues. The breakups are caused by partners crossing racial boundaries, and the dating exposes the difference in courting tactics, depending on the girl's color. On the island, race is a factor as well, and skin color is an issue. In "Ysrael," Rafa insults his younger brother by calling him a Haitian: "Unless, of course, he was mad and then he had about five hundred routines he liked to lay on me. Most of them had to do with complexion, my hair, the size of my lips. It's the Haitian, he'd say to his buddies. Hey Señor Haitian, Mami found you on the border and only took you in because she felt sorry for *you*" (*Drown* 5). The protagonist, in fact, suffers from a self-hating image. He does not like the way he looks, wanting to avoid any connection to his African roots.

Díaz incorporates brief historical points in his stories, especially the United States invasion of 1965, from which the mother survives with scars to prove it. The Trujillo dictatorship is also mentioned in the story "Negocios." As the narrator recreates Ramón's first year in the United States, he describes his father's fastidiousness with clothes and his pride in his appearance, which made him look more like a foreigner than a *mojado* (wetback). In the story "Negocios," El General (Trujillo's nickname) and his daughter's name, Flor de Oro, function as code names. The story also portrays life in the Dominican Republic. The *abuelo* sits on his rocker, watching the daily activity of the street. The *abuelo* serves as the oral link to the past. The street names serve as historical markers, Sumner Welles, for instance, the American ambassador who fully supported Trujillo, and Duarte, one of the Haitian liberators of the Dominican Republic. Other things mentioned are the Guardia Civil uniforms and the divisive racism between the Haitians and Dominicans: "The only way we could have been poorer was to have lived in the campo or to have been Haitian immigrants" (*Drown* 70).

References to being in the United States are juxtaposed with memories of the homeland. In "Fiesta, 1980," the mother believes that all American things from furniture to appliances are intrinsically evil. Yet North American clothes are identified frequently as being a sign of success, North American food as making individuals healthier, adding weight to their poverty-stricken frames. The narrator notices that his mother looks healthier now. Despite the advantages of being in the United States, many of the characters still romanticize the Dominican Republic. Although poverty characterized Yunior's family while they were in Santo Domingo, when they are all together in the United States, a sense of longing and pride in the homeland emerges. In "Fiesta, 1980," as the adults get progressively more drunk, they dance and shout "!Quisqueya!" the native name for the Dominican Republic (*Drown* 40). The narrator's neighborhood, Washington Heights, or Quisqueya Heights, as some now call it (Winn 585), is to the Dominican Republic what Spanish Harlem is to Puerto Rico and Miami to Cuba. Díaz, like other authors in this book, pays homage to the little Dominican Republic, reinvented and re-created on the mainland. Salsa and merengue, the dance of Puerto Rico and the Dominican Republic respectively, is heard on the streets all day long. Spanglish is the spoken language of this mainland homeland. Díaz incorporates Spanglish without any italics. Mostly his Spanglish is a mixture of slang and curse words. He is not concerned with translating the Spanish terms for his readers. In this sense, like many writers included here, he emphasizes that Spanglish is the language of Latinos on the mainland and should no longer be considered a foreign language.

FURTHER SUGGESTED READINGS

Works by Junot Díaz

Díaz, Junot. "The Brief Wondrous Life of Oscar Wao." *The New Yorker* (25 Dec. 2000 & 1 Jan. 2001): 98–117.

———. "Introduction." *The Beacon Best of 2001: Great Writing by Women and Men of All Colors and Cultures*. New York: Beacon Press, 2001.

———. "Nilda." *The New Yorker* (4 Oct. 1999): 92–97.

———. *Drown*. New York: Riverhead Books, 1997.

Other Suggested Readings

Paravisini-Gebert, Lizabeth. "Junot Díaz's *Drown*: Revisiting 'Those Mean Streets.' " *U.S. Latino Literature: A Critical Guide for Students and Teachers*. Westport, CT: Greenwood Press, 2000.

Perez, Loida Maritza. *Geographies of Home*. New York: Penguin Group, 2000.

Rocco, Claudia. "Nothing Sorry about Success of Author Junot Díaz." <http://www.suburbanchicagonews.com>, April 10, 2002.

Rosario, Nelly. *Song of the Water Saints*. New York: Pantheon Books, 2002.

Winn, Peter. *Americas: The Changing Face of Latin America and the Caribbean*. Berkeley and Los Angeles: University of California Press, 1992.

Zeledón, Maximo. "Dominican Dominion." <http://www.fronteramag.com/issue5/Diaz/index.htm>, April 8, 2002.

Chapter 5

The Fiction of Cristina García: Dreaming in Cuban *(1992) and* The Agüero Sisters *(1997)*

Cristina García was born in Havana, Cuba, in 1958. In 1961, her family fled Fidel Castro's revolution, emigrating to Brooklyn, New York. García did not return to Cuba until 1984, more than twenty-five years after her family left. At that time, she reestablished contact with her mother's family, especially her maternal grandmother, who had remained behind after the revolution. From her grandmother's stories, García learned about a different side of the revolution and its effects on her family members. The discovery of the differing views of the revolution within her own family was a major thematic force behind her first novel, *Dreaming in Cuban* (1992). Upon the birth of her daughter, Pilar, García began returning regularly to Cuba so that her daughter would learn about all aspects of her Cuban heritage. García completed her undergraduate degree at Barnard, where she discovered her passion for literature. Her passion was put on hold, however, as she had already been accepted into the master's program in political science at Johns Hopkins University. After graduating from Johns Hopkins in 1981, she worked for *Time* magazine from 1983–1990. She served as a reporter, correspondent, and finally bureau chief in Miami, Florida, for a year before she quit her job to become a writer. She had loved the unexpected assignments, meeting different people, and learning about their cultures. Reporting trained her to focus on the small and precise details of a story, a skill that has served her well in her fiction.

The stories García covered for *Time* magazine, in addition to her own experiences with the Miami Cubans and her visits back to Cuba, inspired her to create her own story, captured fictionally in *Dreaming in Cuban*. Her novel, a finalist for the 1992 National Book Award, describes how the Cuban Revolution affected three generations of Del Pino women. Although the novel can be read as a microcosm for the contemporary political history of Cuba, namely the Castro dictatorship, García insists this is not what she had in mind. Her goal was to closely examine how women adapted to the disruption of their families after the revolution. The alienation and separation that the del Pino family suffers because of political differences is a theme that García returned to five years later in *The Agüero Sisters* (1997). Her second novel, like the first, describes a family saga focused on the Agüero sisters, but it also includes a more sweeping historical framework, reaching back to the War of 1898, but also to the traditional way of rolling a Cuban cigar. García has published short stories about Cuban exiles and has coedited a collection of photographs titled *Cars of Cuba*. This last book points to the well-known fact that Cuba harbors some of the best Fords and Chevys from the 1940s and 1950s, the years of the Batista regime: "When Fidel Castro marched into Havana on New Year's Day of 1959, nearly thirty-five years ago," she writes, "he could not have imagined that his triumph would ultimately create the greatest living American car museum in the world, a hunk of Americana not even available in the U.S." (Introduction 7).

García's fiction expands on Cuban identity and the official version of Cuban history. Her work illustrates the peculiarities, the idiosyncrasies, the successes and failures of the Cuban family, both on the island and the mainland. At the same time, she rewrites the national history of Cuba from a female point of view. García's principal goal in writing is to create a more complex picture of Cuba and its people on both sides of the Strait. In describing what motivated her to write *Dreaming in Cuban,* García says:

I felt that I was trying to look at Cuba in the round. For me, it was not black and white. I'm presenting different points of view that I don't think can be categorized in the official polarization that exists in the Cuban context. Literarily, I'm trying to complicate the picture. . . . The more you can encompass the complexity of a situation, the closer to the truth you get, not the other way around (Kevane and Heredia 76).

García's novels achieve this goal. It would be hard to pinpoint one type of Cuban or an official history of Cuba based on her novels. The Cuban identity has many different shades in her novels, just as the versions of Cuban history vary in her novels, depending on whether or not one is a supporter of the revolution. What stands out, however, is a sense of alienation, a lack of communication, an intransigence among the characters that will only be broken by the characters when they are willing to face the past and how it has divided them. In a sense, it seems like García has been intent on describing Cubans like her, those who do not fit into the tight-knit community found in Miami nor to the Cubans found on the island. García, and her characters, are "other" Cubans.

Dreaming in Cuban, divided into three parts with a total of seventeen chapters, describes the effects of the Cuban Revolution on the del Pino family. García focuses on the politics of Castro's regime as seen through the intergenerational relationship of mother-daughter-granddaughter, Celia, Lourdes and Pilar. On the surface, it appears that the Cuban Revolution caused the family division that the reader discovers as the novel begins in 1972. García develops Celia as a staunch supporter of Castro's revolution, Lourdes as a vehement anti-Castro American immigrant, and Pilar as the granddaughter caught between these two extremes. However, the political extremes that define the characters are largely a result of a personal and familial past, one of loss and abandonment, that haunts each of them. It becomes more apparent that the political choices of the characters are in many ways tied to their personal vendettas against each other. Celia, the matriarch of the Del Pino family sadly remarks about her children, "There is no solace among them, only a past infected with lies" (*Dreaming* 117).

The personal feuds cause political alliances to develop among the characters. Celia and Javier secretly support communism in retaliation against Jorge's distance from them. Lourdes and Jorge, in turn, hate communism largely because it has taken Celia away from them. Luz and Milagro are the young supporters of the revolution largely because they are ostracized from Ivanito and Felicia's intimate world. Pilar stands against her mother, Lourdes, and with Celia. This combination of personal vendettas coupled with political choices creates intractable characters who feel a painful isolation and loneliness. They feel a distance not only between their homeland and themselves, but also between their inner and outer worlds, their family and society, their political ideals and realities. Despite this, as shall be seen, there is a sense of hope for a new family at the end of the novel.

The alienation between characters, their personal and geographical exile, is reflected in the title. *Dreaming in Cuban* aptly captures the world within which the characters live, a self-contained world that they share only with each other, as is the nature of dreams. The novel contains a dream-like quality; there is little direct contact between the characters. Underlying this dream-like quality is language or, more precisely, the inability of the characters to understand each other's language. Each character lives within the confines of his or her personal obsessions, unable to reach out to the others. When they do attempt to communicate in order to better understand their circumstances, it is through alternative mediums: Celia communicates telepathically with Pilar and writes letters that she never sends to her Spanish lover; Lourdes communicates with the spirit of her dead father; Felicia communicates through *santería* (popular folk religion that combines worship of Catholic saints and African gods); Luz and Milagro speak a cryptic language that their mother cannot penetrate. Ivanito, who has a fascination with words because they seem to just 'click' inside him, understands and mimics Felicia's poetically deranged language. Pilar believes her art will create "a unique language, obliterate the clichés" (*Dreaming* 139). Celia, meanwhile, criticizes Pilar's Spanish, deeming it "no longer hers." Lourdes understands the world only in black and white terms and, as she herself says, "has no patience for dreamers, for people who live between black and white" (*Dreaming* 129). Jorge cannot understand Celia, just as Felicia's daughters do not understand her, and finally the man who rapes Lourdes inscribes something on her body that she can't understand but must carry with her for the rest of her life.

The chapters are narrated in either the first person or the third person. The first-person voice is employed by the following characters: Celia, in her love letters to Gustavo; Celia's grandchildren; Pilar; Luz; Ivanito; and Herminia Delgado, the only non-del Pino voice in the novel, the daughter of a *babalawo*, "a high priest of *santería*" (*Dreaming* 183). García's choice of first person points to interesting issues in the novel: Celia's letters reflect a time before the revolution, whereas the grandchildren reflect a set of voices that are post-revolution. Meanwhile, Herminia's voice represents the black African *santera*, someone shunned in Cuban society as a *bruja*.

In addition to the alternating narrative voices, García archives Celia's letters as a way to reveal information about the characters and Cuba's past. Celia's letters to Gustavo Sierra de Armas, her long-lost Spanish lover with whom she had a romantic liaison before marrying Jorge del Pino, date from November 11, 1934 to January 11, 1959. They not only supply the reader with pre-Castro history—the Fulgencio Batista regime, Cuba's poverty, and inequality—but also, and more importantly, they describe the del Pino history before Castro. The letters furnish the reader with a much-needed history of the genealogical beginnings of madness in the del Pino family, starting with Celia's own mother. At the same time, the reader witnesses through Celia's eyes the turbulent years of the Batista regime, the poverty and corruption that assailed the island during Batista's last years, and the excitement and mobilization that led to Castro's revolution.

Dreaming in Cuban (1992)

PART I, "ORDINARY SEDUCTIONS" (APRIL–AUGUST 1972)

Part I, made up of seven chapters, opens with the death of Jorge del Pino, Celia's husband. His death serves as the catalyst that induces the characters to question the choices they have made before and after the revolution. With Jorge's death, the remaining characters begin a physical and emotional journey toward each other that ends with a final reunion in Cuba. The seven chapters, many of which are divided into two narrative voices, depict the estranged relationships in the del Pino family. It focuses on the mother-daughter relationships like those of Celia-Lourdes, Celia-Felicia, Lourdes-Pilar, and Felicia and her twin daughters, Luz and Milagro.

The first chapter, "Ocean Blue," opens in Cuba with Celia guarding the coast from another Bay of Pigs and fantasizing about being feted and seduced by Castro. While she is fulfilling her patriotic duties, she spots her husband's spirit emerging from the ocean. Her husband, Jorge del Pino, who had gone to the United States to be treated for stomach cancer, had died. The second section of the chapter focuses on Felicia's discovery of her father's death. Not even questioning when her mother tells her that she has seen the spirit of her father, she bemoans the fact that her father did not "visit" her. Felicia is convinced by her *santera* friend Herminia that she should attempt to see him and make peace with him before his spirit leaves. Felicia agrees, and what follows is a traditional scene of *santería*, with freshly slaughtered roosters and shrines—a shrine both to Cuban African gods like Oggún, patron of metals and Elleguá, god of the crossroads, and to Catholic saints.

Chapter 2, "Going South," takes place in New York and is divided between Lourdes Puente and her daughter Pilar, who have been living in Brooklyn, New York, since 1961. Like Celia and Felicia, Lourdes, upon learning of her father's death, reminisces about the past and, specifically about 1936, the year she was born. The year she was born coincides with the year that Celia is institutionalized. Lourdes now wears a size 26 and owns a bakery. She has named it Yankee Doodle, which is symbolic of her full adoption of North American values. Her insatiable appetites for both sex and sweets are an attempt to fill a void that she doesn't quite understand but knows is directly linked to her past and to Cuba.

The second section of this chapter introduces the thirteen-year-old Pilar. In a first-person narration, Pilar describes her desire to escape to Cuba, away from her domineering mother and her distant father who, she discovers, is having an affair. Born in 1959, eleven days after Castro came into power, Pilar remembers the last time she saw her grandmother, in 1961, when she was two years old. Ever since her departure from Cuba, Pilar has been able to communicate telepathically with her grandmother.

"The House on Palmas Street," the third chapter, returns to Cuba and describes Celia's past in more detail, both through her reminiscences as she awaits her two granddaughters and through her first set of letters to Gustavo. The letters, which date from 1935–1940, describe the particulars of Celia's personal life: marriage and children, institutionalization, electric-shock therapy, and her recollections of her life with *Tía Alicia* after her own mother abandoned her. These letters not only form the nexus of a disturbed family history, but also describe Celia's budding sense of social justice. Her last observation, about the state of Cuba, alludes to the Batista dictatorship, during which only the wealthy enjoyed economic prosperity while the rest suffered from dire poverty. This observation will flourish in her second set of letters. Celia, now more dissatisfied with Cuba's social stratification, becomes interested in helping to perpetrate social change.

Chapter 5 describes Pilar's arrival in Miami, where she hopes to find a way to Cuba. In addition to the initial description of Pilar's journey, her arrival in Miami provides García with the opportunity to describe the losses of one particular Miami Cuban family. The Puente family, which Lourdes marries into, lives as if at any moment they will be able to return to Cuba. They have not adapted to the United States, and it is apparent that they will remain paralyzed by their impending return to the island, the discussion of which occupies all of their time. The second half of the chapter describes Lourdes's encounter with her father's spirit, forty days after his burial. Jorge and Lourdes begin a series of evening conversations that also begin Lourdes's journey toward reconciliation with her daughter and with Cuba.

Chapter 6 supplies the reader with Felicia's personal history, her delusions, her marriage to Hugo, who abuses her, and her relationship with Ivanito. The second half focuses on Ivanito, who describes his mother and her attempt at suicide, as well as her attempt to kill him. The third section of this chapter describes Celia's attempt to help Felicia and provides us with further details of her past, for instance her mother's abandonment of her and her childhood with her *Tía* Alicia in Havana.

The last chapter contains Celia's second set of letters, written between 1942 and 1949. These letters reflect a more globally conscious Celia, concerned about the nation-making that emerges after World War II, concerned about the way the world is being carved up (*Dreaming* 99) while also reflecting a waning love for Gustavo. In effect, political concerns and the revolution will replace her previous passion for Gustavo.

PART II, "IMAGINING WINTER" (1974–1980)

If Jorge's death forced the characters to reminisce and to question their past and present circumstances, Felicia's death toward the end of Part II motivates the final reunion of the characters. Part II begins in Cuba two years later, 1974, and ends with Felicia's death in 1980. The first chapter, "The Meaning of Shells," deftly captures the different organizations that Castro implemented in order to control his new revolutionary society, in which everything was to be done for the revolution and nothing against it. Divided between Felicia and Celia, this chapter describes in fascinating detail a group of social misfits in the "Social Disgrace Unit" and the People's Court, over which Celia presides. Felicia, after trying to kill herself and Ivanito, is sent to camp to become a "New Socialist Woman." The boot-camp sings common slogans like "Fatherland or death" (Patria o muerte). Those in Felicia's camp are deemed social misfits or malcontents. The term misfit applies to a huge spectrum of Cuban citizens: men with long hair, anyone who listens to American jazz, people who say grace at the dinner table, people who believe in the church, homosexuals, intellectuals, and, of course individuals who do not support Castro.

Meanwhile, Celia, who fulfills her revolutionary duty as guard and judge, presides over the People's Court in which she decides the fate of her community members. Although proud of her responsibility, after 193 cases Celia only feels disillusionment; she realizes that the citizens of her neighborhood view this revolutionary task, and community courts, as an opportunity to view a soap opera. The last section, which takes place in 1975, is a first-person narration by Luz, one of Felicia's twin daughters, who describes their troubled childhood with their mother, Felicia. Luz tells about how Felicia burns Hugo, their father, with a rag on fire, permanently disfiguring him. Luz and Milagro are secretly reconciled with their father in defiance of Felicia.

"Enough Attitude," the second chapter, returns to life in the United States and to Lourdes and Pilar, who is now seventeen. The mother and daughter are further alienated from each other. Lourdes has joined the auxiliary police, embracing authority, whereas Pilar has become a punk, rebel artist who embraces Lou Reed. Despite their separation, this chapter describes the first step toward reconciliation; Lourdes invites Pilar to paint something for the grand opening of Lourdes's second Yankee Doodle Bakery. Pilar paints the Statue of Liberty in punk fashion. Although Lourdes's clients are aghast, Lourdes protects her daughter's painting. At that moment, we understand the strong bond between mother and daughter.

Chapter 3, "Baskets of Water," includes narrations from Ivanito, Felicia, and Celia in Cuba. Ivanito's narration describes life as a student in Cuba, Felicia's section describes her disappearance and next two marriages, and Celia's section describes the return and subsequent disappearance of her suffering son Javier from Czechoslovakia. The chapter that follows contains another set of Celia's letters, which date from 1950 to 1955. They describe family events, like the death of her mother-in-law and the antagonistic relationship between Jorge and their son Javier, as well as political events, such as Fulgencio Batista's staged military coup of 1952. It also conveys Celia's growing awareness of the disparity in economic levels in Cuba and her nascent activism in the Orthodox Party, the political party opposed to Fulgencio Batista (Partido Ortodoxo, Partido del Pueblo Cubano), of which Fidel Castro was an active member. She describes Fidel's momentous attack on the second-largest army base in Moncada. Although the attack failed, it gave hope to people like Celia, who wanted Batista to be ousted.

Chapter 5, "A Matrix Light," returns to the United States and begins with Lourdes in 1977. Now that her father has died, Lourdes's obsession with food manifests itself in starvation, in the desire to feel empty and hollow. She has successfully lost the 118 pounds she gained upon the arrival of her father in New York. Lourdes continues her evening conversations with her father, who has now been dead for five years. Pilar, meanwhile, is an art student in college, "still waiting for my life to begin" (*Dreaming* 179).

The chapter that describes Felicia's death and initiation into *santería,* "God's Will," is divided in terms of point of view between Herminia, the only non-del Pino voice in the novel, and Ivanito, Felicia's son. It is an important chapter in that it includes the voice of a black African, Cuban woman, Herminia, whose father practiced *santería*. With this voice, García is able to incorporate and highlight some of the racial issues that characterize Cuba, racial issues many times ignored or dismissed by Cubans as nonexistent. Herminia is Felicia's best friend because Felicia is "the only person I've known who didn't see color" (*Dreaming* 184). "Daughters of Changó," which refers to the Afro-Cuban Changó, god of fire and lightning, depicts the decision made by Pilar, and followed reluctantly by Lourdes, to return to Cuba. In this chapter, Lourdes's father reveals that he attempted and succeeded in killing Celia's spirit, in order to punish her for loving Gustavo, her Spanish lover, more than she loved him. Jorge's parting words are a mandate to Lourdes, "Please return and tell your mother everything, tell her I'm sorry. I love you, *mi hija* [my daughter]" (*Dreaming* 197). Pilar, now twenty-one years old, finds herself empty and "dried up inside." She is drawn to a *botánica,* a store the sells herbs, potions, and charms to aid in *santera* rites. The elderly owner of the store immediately notes that she is a daughter of Changó and prescribes bitter baths for nine days, promising that on the ninth day she will know what to do. On her way home, Pilar is sexually assaulted by three young boys, which creates a parallel between herself and Lourdes. Lourdes escapes as far north as she can after her rape; Pilar desires nothing more than to return to her homeland after being assaulted. Celia's letters from 1956–1958 end Part II, as those from 1942–1949 did Part I. The letters again narrate both family and political events. One of these events is the engagement of her daughter Lourdes to Rufino Puente, who is from one of the wealthiest families in Havana, staunch supporters of Batista and of the United States. The imminence of the revolution creates tension in Celia's home, and Jorge fears losing his job with an American company. Celia, who believes in the revolution, tells him that "there'll be more jobs for everyone when they throw that thief out of the palace" (*Dreaming* 209).

PART III, "LANGUAGES LOST" (1980)

Composed of only two chapters, Part III describes the reunion between Celia, Lourdes, Pilar, and Ivanito. Hope, death, and resolution characterize these two final chapters. Lourdes reconciles herself with the violent acts that remind her of her last days in Cuba, and Celia ends her own life. Pilar, who realizes she cannot live within the social restrictions of the regime, now knows that she belongs in New York, "not *instead* of here, but *more* than here" (*Dreaming* 236; author's italics). For the first time, Lourdes and Pilar act together and help Ivanito escape to the United States through the Peruvian embassy, thus creating a new Cuban family.

The novel closes with Celia's last letter, dated January 11, 1959, in which she announces the birth of the revolution and that of her granddaughter Pilar.

CULTURAL ELEMENTS

The Cuban Revolution serves as the historical and cultural framework of the novel. Those who supported the revolution anticipated a host of changes that would allow a more integrated and equal society. Afro-Cubans, women, and the poor *campesinos* believed in the social and political changes that Castro promised: participation at a political, social, and economic level; educational opportunities; and the betterment of social welfare and health care. The anticipation of the revolution and its denouement, witnessed in Celia's letters, represented a new future and hope for many Cubans. Castro's triumphant entry into Habana (Havana) was matched by the excitement and pride of much of the population who, for the first time in Cuban history—and especially since the War of 1898—had successfully completed their revolutionary goals. They had overthrown the repressive and United States-backed Batista regime without being thwarted by the United States (Pérez, Jr. 314). Most landowners, like Rufino Puente's family, upper-class members of society, and professionals fled the island when Castro nationalized private property and enterprises and then redistributed them. This migration, known as the "Golden Exile," depleted much of Cuba's intellectual and professional sector. But the Cubans who remained, those who believed in the revolution and those who simply could not leave, were quickly trained and versed in the revolutionary ideology of "El Líder," as Castro was called, as well as educated to fill the professional gap.

García's novel portrays that historical victory, but it also describes the somewhat absurd outcome of the Cuban revolution twelve years later, from 1972–1980, blatantly contrasting the ideals of the revolution with its deceptions. Castro and the revolutionary party's ideology grew increasingly strict; newspapers, religion, music, and art experienced censorship, and poets, homosexuals, and anyone who did not passionately accept the new ideology were censured. All social organizations that emerged were created in order to serve the revolution and its needs. No one was allowed freedom of thought, economic gain, or cultural expression that did not validate the party line. The ideals of the revolution were to be honored and supported by all Cubans. In this respect, all employment had some revolutionary component. The novel's opening scene, which takes place in 1972, demonstrates just how preposterous and, perhaps, surreal the revolution had become, when we witness Celia in her revolutionary role as coast guard. While she fulfills her revolutionary duty of protecting the coast from another Bay of Pigs, she fantasizes about being seduced by Castro. In the hopes of this seduction, she always dresses in her best clothes, wears red lipstick, and darkens the mole on her cheek.

The time frame of the novel is linked to important phases of revolutionary activity on the island. The seventies have been termed "The Decade of Institutionalization," and this is portrayed in detail in Part II of García's novel (Suchlicki 173). Fidel created a new language to describe the organizations that supported the people in their revolutionary struggle. García mentions a few: those who pull weeds are named "The Mechanized Offensive Brigade"; young teachers are called "Fighters for Learning"; students working in the fields are the "Juvenile Column of the Centenary"; literacy volunteers are dubbed "The Fatherland or Death Brigade" (*Dreaming* 108). There is a "Social Disgrace Unit" for social misfits, drug addicts, and homosexuals. The "Committee for the Defense of the Revolution" spies on people and files complaints against those behaving in an unrevolutionary way. A new way of addressing people is also created. Instead of *don* or *doña*, the Spanish prefix that meant gentleman and lady, all people are referred to with a new prefix, *compañera* or *compañero*, comrade of equal status in the revolution. *Compañera* Celia's revolutionary duties—a national guard, a community judge, a sugar-cane cutter—might seem strange to a reader who does not understand the social changes that took place after the Cuban Revolution. Employment was reshaped to serve the nation and the revolution. No employment allowed for personal gain, but rather served to further the ideals of the revolution. Other cultural elements were reshaped as well; food, music, religion, and family were reinscribed within the framework of the revolution. For example, food on the island now existed only in rations. Music and art could only exist if they served the revolution, something that Pilar refused to accept. Religious practices were banned under Castro because they were seen as subversive elements; we witness Felicia and Herminia practicing *santería* in secret. Family must remain united for the revolution or, as a comrade tells Felicia, one's own daughters will turn one in. Family breaks apart not only because of the personal, but because Castro's regime provides no room whatsoever for a middle ground. "Socialismo o muerte" (Socialism or death), are the only two choices allowed Cuban citizens. Lourdes imagines changing the slogan to "Socialismo es muerte" (Socialism is death), to describe what the revolution has done to Cuba.

The novel ends in 1980, with the takeover of the Peruvian embassy by thousands of Cubans who were attempting to leave the island. In March

1980, six men crashed a stolen bus into the Peruvian embassy. Roughly 10,000 Cubans fled to the embassy for refuge and eventual exile to other places. Castro, a month later, announced that any Cuban who wanted to would be allowed to leave. The Cubans and their departure became known as the "Mariel Boatlift"; more than 125,000 Cubans left from the port of Mariel to the United States and elsewhere (Rogozinski 244). García conflates the two events, the bus crash and Castro's declaration of free passage, ending the novel in April with Castro's announcement that anyone could emigrate from Cuba. The departure reflects the exhaustion with the revolution that led many to create a new life outside of Castro's Cuba. Lourdes and Pilar secure Ivanito's departure from Cuba at this point, adopt him, and thus create a new family.

From the opening of the novel, the reader is made aware of how neatly divided the two worlds that characterize the novel are—the communist dictatorship of Cuba, and the democracy and capitalism of the United States. Throughout the novel, and as revealed through the characters, Cuba and the United States stand at opposite ends of the political spectrum. Celia, guarding the coast from another Bay of Pigs, makes immediate historical reference to the contentious relationship between Cuba and the United States. In revolutionary Cuba, the United States stands as the ultimate enemy that might, at any moment, attack Cuba again as it did in 1961 in the Bay of Pigs. In fact, the categorization of all elements of society in the name of the revolution stands in stark contrast to the liberties and opportunities that characterize the United States. The strictures on food, music, religion, and employment that exist in Cuba contrast sharply with the choices available to Lourdes, Rufino, and Pilar in Brooklyn. Lourdes lives in a world of excess: capitalism, food, sex, and opinions. In the United States, capitalism replaces the socialism she has left behind in Cuba. An excess of rich pastries replaces the ration coupon book that limits the food available to Cubans on the island. Punk music and art replace slogans that proclaim support for Castro's revolution. Pilar, who grows up with her mother's excess, but who remembers her grandmother will, in the end, mediate the two extremes.

At the same time that Castro institutionalized all aspects of Cuban society, he expanded gender roles, allowing women to participate in the revolution on several levels. The fact that Celia performs a job that could save Cuba from another Bay of Pigs, or from deserters, is laughable except that Celia believes she is a direct participant in the revolution. She guards the north coast from either *gusanos* (worms), a derogatory term invented by Castro to insult the deserters of the revolution, or from another Bay of Pigs. Celia also enjoys her role as the civilian judge of her town, Santa Teresa del Mar. Before the revolution she would have been expected to "Sway endlessly on her wicker swing, old before her time" (111) or to take care of her grandchildren while waiting to die. Lourdes also criticizes the old patriarchal gen-

der roles, where women are supposed to remain at home cooking and rais-
ing the children.

The identity of the characters is affected by the Castro regime. Through
Celia, Felicia, and the three grandchildren, Ivanito, Luz and Milagro, readers witness life under the Castro regime—telephone outages, food rationing,
revolutionary activities, the change in title to *compañera and compañero*, and
more—and its ultimate effects. In addition, each character relates to the revolution as if it were another character. Celia, throughout the novel, remains
an ardent supporter, despite the fact that her revolutionary ideals have been
replaced by fantasies about Castro. Yet, by the end of the novel she realizes
that her political passion blinded her to the fracturing of her family. In the
end, she commits suicide. Felicia is a complete skeptic with regard to the
revolution, does not buy into the ideology, and escapes to *santería*. Felicia
reflects a segment of the population that lives within the restrictions of the
revolution—food stamps, boot camp, and so on—but does not accept the
ultimate goal, "Socialismo o muerte." Felicia, in the end, becomes initiated
into *santería* with the help of her friend Herminia, whose father is a high
priest, a *babalow*. *Santería*, a syncretic mix of African pagan gods and
Catholic saints, literally means "in the way of the saints" because African
slaves would place statues of the pagan gods in front of those of Catholic
saints. Practitioners of the African Yoruban religion also equalized Catholic
saints with those in their own religion. Eleggua, for example, the "god of
paths," was equated to a Catholic saint. Although it was officially outlawed
by Castro, many continued to worship in *santería*. Even high-ranking
Castro officials would seek advice from *babalows*.

Felicia's friendship with Herminia also presents a picture of the Afro-
Cuban segment of the population. Not only do we learn about *santería*, but
also, through Herminia, about the historical suppression of Afro-Cubans.
Herminia offers a different perspective on the Castro regime and the exclu-
sion and inclusion of the Afro-Cuba race in Cuban history. (A similar tactic
is employed by Julia Alvarez with the first-person narration of the Haitian
maid Chucha, who practices in voodoo.) She recognizes the subjectivity of
history. Herminia wonders why the Little War of 1912, during which many
blacks were killed because of their color, is simply a footnote in history
books. She rhetorically asks the reader, "Why, then, should I trust anything
I read? I trust only what I see, what I know with my heart, nothing more"
(*Dreaming* 185). From Herminia's point of view, the revolution has
changed things for black people. Instead of mopping floors for white
women, she is a supervisor in a factory, something almost impossible to
imagine before Castro. However, she notes that the patriarchal system, led
by Castro, remains largely in place.

Luz and Milagro do not undergo any change; they remain supporters of
the revolution until the end of the novel. They are the generation born
under and completely indoctrinated into the Castro regime. Their schooling

serves the revolution. They know no other way of life. Their brother is somehow saved from this indoctrination, partially because of his relationship to Felicia but also because his love of language leads him to seek knowledge outside of the regime. In a transgressive manner, he secretly listens to the radio stations that he can access from the United States, which broadcast programs like that of Wolfman Jack.

In addition to the cultural elements that emerge on the island as a result of the strictures of the Castro regime, García portrays the peculiarities of the exile community in New York and Miami. Lourdes emerges as a fanatical capitalist, a consummate consumer, and an over-acculturated American in her reaction to the revolution. She believes in immigration and passionately embraces the opportunity to reinvent herself (*Dreaming* 73). Lourdes, like her mother, becomes vigilant, and is an auxiliary policewoman. While Celia guards the beach from "Yanqui" invasions, Lourdes guards her neighborhood, but in order to fight the Communists "when the time came" (*Dreaming* 132). Her father's spirit encourages her to join the enforcement order in imitation of Fidel. Celia and her daughter embrace the role of law and order, but to fight opposing forces. Lourdes and Celia represent the two extremes of Castro's regime. Lourdes, who bakes Uncle Sam marzipan pastries and wants her daughter to paint a big painting, "like the Mexicans do, but pro-American," travels to Cuba to proselytize to everyone about the opportunities in the United States. Her husband Rufino, on the other hand, cannot adapt to their life in the United States: "There was a part of him that could never leave the *finca* (farm) or the comfort of its cycles, and this diminished him for any other life. He could not be transplanted" (*Dreaming* 129).

Pilar is the bicultural character at the crossroads. Elements that characterize Pilar are typical of the collective Cuban exile community: "Longing for roots, a sense of displacement, the persistence of memory, a need to replay history and an idealization of Cuba itself" (Poey and Suarez 11). In some ways, Pilar is a typical American teenager enjoying the freedom of the mainland. She embraces punk, she rebels against her parents and, most importantly, she is able to study art. However, Pilar is also haunted by her severed roots. Like Yolanda in *García Girls,* Pilar represents the Cuban exile not old enough to fully understand why she lives in exile; she is distrustful of the past her mother describes and is constantly in search of her roots. Pilar retains a nostalgic hold on the island in order to preserve her sense of identity. When in Miami, ninety miles from Cuba, Pilar is not sure whether either Brooklyn or Cuba is her home: "If I could only see Abuela Celia again, I'd know where I belonged" (*Dreaming* 58). Pilar does not adopt either political stance and, thus, does not have a full sense of self until her return to Cuba. Pilar feels like "a new me sprouts and dies every day" (*Dreaming* 135). Her telepathic communication with her grandmother dies when she is about fourteen years old and, for her, so does Cuba: "Every day Cuba fades a little more inside me, my grandmother fades a little more inside me. And there's only my imagination where our history should be" (*Dreaming* 138).

The return to the homeland for Pilar and Lourdes is very different than the return home is for Yolanda, although both journeys have a similar outcome. As soon as they arrive on the island, Pilar and Lourdes witness the propaganda, the advertising of the revolution as if it were a cigarette. Yolanda in *García Girls* can better understand the past, present and future at the end of the novel, Pilar on returning to Cuba, has gained the ability to "glimpse scraps of the future" and, more importantly, to tell the story. But it is her love of art that enables her to witness the reality of Cuba. During the six days that Lourdes and Pilar are in Cuba, Pilar asks her grandmother about the art of the revolution. Her grandmother responds that art is fine so long as it supports the revolution. Pilar realizes that she cannot survive in Castro's Cuba because, in her mind, "Art is the ultimate revolution" (*Dreaming* 235). At this point, she decides that she belongs in Brooklyn.

Pilar understands that Cuba is an island unto itself that cannot be understood by her, that does not even understand itself anymore. As Catherine Moses wrote, "Cuba exists in an alternate reality; it is another world from another time. Mostly cut off from the Western world for more than three decades, it has evolved along its own path. It has become a curious mixture of Spanish Caribbean, socialist ideals gone awry, memories of what was, and a desperate need to survive" (Moses 2). Pilar reflects upon this very idea at the end of the novel and says, "Cuba is a peculiar exile, I think, an island-colony. We can reach it by a thirty-minute charter flight from Miami, yet never reach it all" (*Dreaming* 219).

The Agüero Sisters (1997)

The Agüero Sisters narrates the story of estranged sisters Reina, who is forty-eight years old, and Constancia, who is fifty years old. Reina lives in Cuba when the novel opens and believes in the revolution, although not in a fanatical manner. Constancia is on the verge of moving from Manhattan to Miami with her husband Heberto, and she is a wealthy and successful entrepreneur. Just as in *Dreaming in Cuban*, the sisters are separated because of a troublesome family history and because of the revolution. The family history creates a wedge between the siblings, and the revolution further exacerbates their separation. The contemporary action of the novel, which takes place in a short time frame, a little less than a year (from December 1990 to September 1991), alternates between Cuba and Miami. As in *Dreaming*, in which Celia's letters supplemented the novel with an historical and a familial past, Ignacio Agüero's diary functions as an archive that holds important information and crucial answers about his and his daughters' past. Ignacio's diary begins with his birth in 1904 and ends with the murder of his wife,

Blanca Agüero, by his hand in 1950. Constancia and Reina will not be able to resolve their contentious relationship with each other or with the past until they discover Ignacio's diary. The action of the novel begins with Reina in Cuba and Constancia in New York and then Miami, and it ends with Constancia in Habana and Reina in Miami. By the end of the novel, the two have exchanged geographical locations in their need to discover and expose a family and national history made up of lies and secrets.

Dreaming in Cuban roughly covered the seventies and 1980; this novel addresses Castro's Cuba in its thirty-first year of existence. It was a different decade in Castro's ongoing revolution. With the collapse of the Soviet Union, Cuba was at a loss economically. True to his past propensity to create a formal and official name for every social and political event on the island, Castro named this economically bleak decade *el Periódo Especial,* or "the special period." Cubans were asked to work harder and to consume less in order to sustain the ideals of the revolution. The Cuban people reached an unprecedented level of exhaustion. In the interest of survival, a thriving black market arose, where doctors and artisans alike sold their wares, or anything they could think of, in exchange for basics at *ferias.* These open-air markets were not called markets because that would imply the capitalistic exchange of money. *Jineteras* (prostitutes), like Reina's daughter Dulce, also became more common since women sold their bodies in order to escape or to secure staple or luxury items. During this time Fidel was referred to as "'NiNi' (neither nor), meaning neither electricity, nor food, nor water, nor much of anything" (Moses 11).

Constancia Agüero, the older sister, lives in New York but, when the novel opens, is about to move to Miami with her husband, who secretly intends to join a movement that will overthrow Castro. Reina, the younger sister, still lives in Habana. At the opening of the novel, Reina supports the revolution as a fact of life. She is not the fanatical Celia character in García's first novel, but simply the Cuban individual who accepts the revolution. Constancia, meanwhile, thinks little of the revolution and despises the fact that her husband still dreams of overthrowing Castro. The sisters are separated geographically because of the Castro regime but also, as in García's first novel, they are separated emotionally because they each remember a different past about their parents. Constancia is loyal to her father, whereas Reina is loyal to the memory of her mother. What drives a stake through their relationship is the death of their mother, which each daughter remembers differently. Despite their differences in terms of their mother's death/murder, they are joined by their need to seek within each other the memory of the mother that they lost at such a young age. In the end, the desire to seek the truth about their mother forces the sisters to a reconciliation with both their familial and national past.

There are other similarities of plot between *Dreaming in Cuban* and this second novel, including a husband who attempts to (*Dreaming*) or who does (*Sisters*) kill his wife. This fact remains a secret to the daughters until later in life. Both men, Ignacio and Javier, attempt to kill or do kill their wives because of the inaccessibility of the wife. Celia longs for her Spanish lover; Blanca runs off with a mulatto man and has a child, Reina, with him. In addition, Constancia marries Heberto even though she is still "sick with love for his brother," but Heberto, as the narrator says, is incapable of jealousy. Constancia has a close relationship to her father, as did Lourdes. Constancia, obsessed with *milagros* (miracles), was abandoned at five months by her mother; Lourdes was also abandoned by her mother in *Dreaming in Cuban*. The structure of the novel resembles *Dreaming* as well. There are chapters dedicated to the different characters and narrated in either the first or the third person. An archive, Ignacio's diary, provides details of the past. The first-person narrators are Ignacio Agüero, who records the past, and Dulce Fuerte, Reina's daughter, who reflects the present and the generation of children born after the revolution but whose parents were directly involved. The different voices in this novel, as in García's previous novel, serve to enforce the idea that history is composed of a multiplicity of points of view, rather than one monolithic history, like that controlled by Castro.

Part I, "Tropical Disturbances," introduces the reader to the main problems and issues that the characters face. The action takes place during five months, from December 1990 to April 1991, and is interspersed with Ignacio's diary entries. As the title of the part indicates, the characters are set in motion by a "disturbance" that forever changes their lives and leads them to each other. Reina Agüero, an electrician and the daughter conceived out of wedlock, is electrocuted during a routine job. As she recovers in a hospital in Cuba, she realizes that she is exhausted with her life. Her daughter, Dulce, has already left for Spain, seeking a better life, and so Reina moves to Miami to recover physically and emotionally: "Revolutionary dedication goes only so far" (*Sisters* 16). The next chapter describes Reina's sister, Constancia, the older sister at fifty, working in a Manhattan department store, selling cosmetics. She and her husband embody the rich Cuban workers who have been successful in the United States. Soon, she will be moving to Key Biscayne, Florida, with her husband, Heberto, who is sixty-two and ready to retire. Part I ends with the meeting of the two sisters.

"A Common Affliction," the second part, also covers five months, from May 1991 to September 1991. The first chapter opens with Heberto, who joins other Cubans in exile attempting to return to Cuba to overthrow Castro. References are made to the Bay of Pigs and what esteem it holds in the memory of the Cuban exile community, even though it was a failure. The Bay of Pigs, which Castro and Cubans call Victory at Playa Giron, is " 'the first triumph over imperialism in Latin America'—[and] is celebrated annually" (Moses 12). Those who participated in the Kennedy-backed overthrow of the Castro regime were regarded as heroes by many Cuban

Americans. Heberto, unlike his brothers, was not allowed to go because of his wife, and now participates in a second attempt thirty years later. The sixteen chapters continue to develop the characters. Constancia is a successful entrepreneur with *Cuerpo de Cuba* beauty products; Reina is a successful mechanic and is enjoying the luxuries of Miami. During these chapters the sisters seem to merge, to discover each other and then to separate again. The climax occurs in the last chapter when Reina and Constancia take a boat ride together. They confront each other about the past and their memories. Constancia almost drowns Reina, but then decides to rescue her.

The third part is titled, "Coda: A Root in the Dark." A coda, according to the *Oxford English Dictionary*, is "the concluding passage of a piece or movement, usually forming an addition to the basic structure or a concluding event or series of events." Although this part can be characterized as a conclusion, it is also a rebirth and reconciliation for the characters. It traces Constancia's voyage back to Cuba to recover her husband's body, but also to recover the diary.

CULTURAL ELEMENTS

Ignacio's diary anchors the novel in historical events that precede the Castro regime. References in Ignacio's diary are made to the Platt Amendment (the agreement signed by Cuba and the United States after the War of 1898 defining relations and allowing the U.S. Guantánamo Bay), the first President of the newly formed Cuban Republic in 1904, the tradition of the *lectores* (literally readers in the old cigar-rolling factories), who would read from newspapers, novels and political treatises to entertain and educate cigar rollers, and the Spanish ancestry of many Cubans. The framework for Ignacio Agüero's diary is natural history, his profession. When García was asked about the inclusion of Cuba's long-gone natural wonders, she answered: "It was a way of trying to get at Cuban history without necessarily focusing on the watershed of the revolution. B.R./A.R., before revolution and after revolution. I wanted to get away from the gravitational pull of the revolution and look at loss and memory and nostalgia and extinction and myth making through another prism. I wanted a different kind of metaphor. I think the natural history theme was useful that way" (Kevane and Heredia 79). But García's decision to incorporate the natural history and extinction of Cuba's flora and fauna also serves as an allegory: in describing the growing extinction of the plants and birds, as well as that of their natural habitat, García alludes to the growing extinction of a way of life in Cuba. The Castro regime engaged in an extinction of historical facts as it created a new history of lies. Castro, like many dictators, erased a past in order to create a present. With that erasure comes a collective sense of loss, evident in García's characters. Indeed, the theme is relevant to the characters as well. Constancia at one point feels like she herself is extinct, "like the many lost birds her father had lamented over the years, the birds that Cuba could no longer sustain, the birds they'd vainly searched for in the remotest corners of their sacrificed islands" (*Sisters* 179). But, as García points out, the characters avoid extinction by pursuing the truth in the past. Thus, Constancia will return to Cuba and uncover Ignacio's diary, which will then lead to reconciliation and rebirth among the characters.

In addition to the natural history motif, García opens the novel with Ignacio telling a lie about how his wife died. García's main purpose in writing this novel was to examine the lies that had been told about Cuba at a national level. She uses a family history as an allegory for a national one, the lies of the Castro regime are matched by the lies harbored in the Agüero family. In order for Constancia and Reina to free themselves of their past, they must discover the truth.

In terms of culture, there are diverse aspects that García captures with remarkable clarity. The Cuba of the past, for instance, is described by Ignacio in terms of the flora and fauna, the *lectores*. The Cuba of the present is best described by Dulce Fuertes, as an exhaustive life. She best represents the current culture in Cuba, where everything is for sale, even one's own body. When Constancia returns, she quickly adapts to the change Cuba has undergone since she left. She finds that the black market is the driving force and that nothing surprises her. On the island, "it seems that there's been nothing but bartering and bribes" (*Sisters* 290). Constancia also realizes that part of her no longer belongs to the island, her accent and her looks. She is too manicured, and "her obsolete language" betrays her years in Miami. She quickly becomes accustomed to the island bartering, giving her wet suit and flippers in exchange for Heberto's corpse, and not expecting telephone service or water at all times.

Ignacio's diary, which records his birth in 1904 and ends when he kills his wife, contains the cultural elements that distinguish García's second novel from her first. Ignacio's birth coincides with the election and inauguration of the first President of the Republic, Estrada Palma, after the War of 1898. This was a momentous time for Cuba, as it had finally achieved independence from Spain. Ignacio's father, although from Spain, supported Cuba in its independence. The description of Ignacio's father as a tobacco reader, a *lector,* captures not only a lost time but also lost traditions. García describes the custom that characterized most cigar-rolling factories of the nineteenth and early twentieth centuries, where the *tabaqueros* (cigar rollers) rolled tobacco leaves by hand while listening to a *lector* (reader). The *lector* was highly esteemed and would read aloud to the workers, thus educating the laborers. Tobacco rollers were traditionally liberal in that they opposed Spanish colonialism and supported Cuba's independence from Spain. It is said that José Martí's call to arms against Spain arrived in Cuba from New York City rolled in a cigar. The *lector,* the role that Ignacio's father had in the cigar factory, was of utmost importance. Tobacco rollers prided themselves on being a learned force of labor. Newspapers, philosophical and political treatises, religious questions, and classic novels were all read aloud as the cigar rollers worked. They were the enlightened laborers who favored Cuba's independence and the abolition of slavery. Tobacco rollers and tobacco as an industry faced many hardships in the late 1800s and the early 1900s, when sugar became the rival crop. At the time, many cigar rollers left for the United States. This departure marked the beginning of the Cuban community on the mainland, a highly educated and politically active community (Luis 106).

Constancia and her husband represent the diaspora community, the rich community in exile. Constancia's tale of leaving Cuba in a ship includes tales of hardship; she had to bite off a piece of her daughter's heel in order to jolt her back from death on their secret escape by boat from Cuba to Miami, and she had to send her son ahead of her. Reina, who accepts the ideals of the revolution, also reaches a critical point in her life, when she can no longer tolerate them in realistic terms, although she is a supporter of them in theory. Both *Dreaming* and *Sisters* possess a gamut of characters. In *Dreaming*, however, the characters are at both ends of the spectrum, the two extremes; in *Sisters*, the characters are a little more ambivalent. What is of more concern to Reina and Constancia, what takes center stage, is their family history.

Religious references are made as well. *La Virgen de la Caridad del Cobre* is the island's patron saint. The important difference between this Virgen and the Virgin Mary is not only color of skin, for this Virgen has brown skin, but also the way in which she is adored. García describes the medallions, rings, silks, and so on that belong to the people who believe in the Virgen. Her native Yoruban name is Oshún. This Caribbean *Virgen de Guadalupe*, appears in the novel several times. The characters consistently refer to the Cuban African gods, like Oshún, but also to the *Virgen de la Cobre*, who is revered only in Cuba. Rebirth and reconciliation characterize the last section of this novel: Constancia's return and discovery of her father's diary, Dulce's arrival in Miami, the story of Reina's conception, and the final reconciliation of the two sisters when Constancia discovers the bone her mother saved for her and, in turn, saves it for Reina.

FURTHER SUGGESTED READINGS

Works by Cristina García

García, Cristina, Ed. *¡Cubanismo! The Vintage Book of Contemporary Cuban Literature*. New York: Vintage, 2003.

———. *Monkey Hunting*. New York: Knopf, 2003.

———. *The Agüero Sisters*. New York: Knopf, 1997.

————. *Cars of Cuba*. New York: Harry N. Abrams, 1995.

————. *Dreaming in Cuban*. New York: Ballantine Books, (reprinted), 1993.

Other Suggested Readings

Lamazares, Yvonne. *Sugar Island*. Boston and New York: Houghton Mifflin, 2000.

Luis, William. *Dance Between Two Cultures: Latino Caribbean Literature Written in the United States*. Nashville and London: Vanderbilt University Press, 1997.

Menendez, Ana. *In Cuba I Was A German Shepherd*. New York: Grove Press, 2002.

Moses, Catherine. *Real Life in Castro's Cuba*. New York: Scholarly Resources, 2002.

Poey, Delia and Virgil Suarez, Eds. *Little Havana Blues: A Cuban American Literary Anthology*. Houston: Arte Público Press, 1996.

Valdes, Zoe. *Yocandra in the Paradise of Nada: A Novel of Cuba*. Trans. Sabina Cienfuegos. New York: Arcade Publishing, 1997.

Chapter 6

The Fiction of Oscar Hijuelos: The Mambo Kings Play Songs of Love (1989)

O scar Hijuelos was born in Manhattan in 1951 of Cuban parentage. His parents had left Cuba for New York in the 1940s and settled in Spanish Harlem. Hijuelos was distanced from the tight-knit community of Miami Cubans, who practically define life for Cubans in the United States. In this respect, Hijuelos has said, "In New York, I live in a much more fragmented world in the sense that I belong to many communities and at the same time not solidly to any one" (Bowman 1). Hijuelos attended public schools in New York. He then went on to the Bronx Community College, and finally to the City College of New York, from which he received his B.A. and M.A. in English and Writing. While at City College, he studied with writers like Susan Sontag, Joseph Heller, and Donald Bartheleme. After college, he continued to write while working at different jobs. He also played in jazz bands in New York. His first novel, *Our House in the Last World*, was published in 1983. This fictional autobiography stems from Hijuelos's childhood and contains many autobiographical elements: Spanish was spoken in his home; Hijuelos's father worked as a cook in a hotel, was an alcoholic and died young; his mother wrote poetry; and Hijuelos, like his protagonist Héctor, was hospitalized for a long enough time to learn English and to lose the ability to converse fluently in Spanish. His next work, *The Mambo Kings Play Songs of Love*, published in

1989, received the Pulitzer Prize in 1990. Following his success, he wrote *The Fourteen Sisters of Emilio Montez* (1993), *Mr. Ives' Christmas* (1995), *Empress of the Splendid Season* (1999), and *A Simple Habana Melody (from when times were good)* (2002). Hijuelos currently teaches English at Hofstra University.

Hijuelos distinguishes himself from many contemporary Latino novelists in that the overall impulse of his novels, with the exception of *Our House*, does not stem from the conflict between the homeland and the mainland, between the old and new, between the bicultural and bilingual identity. Rather, it stems from the inner torment that the characters experience. In speaking about his work, Hijuelos describes himself as a "psychological lyricist." By this he means that he writes more from the interior of a character through which he, or the character, can "convey an outer world through the vision of the inner world. But I also try to approach human beings from the point of view of the caprices of their psychology" (Harmon 43). Most of Hijuelos's novels reflect this. He pays intense attention to the inner observations, reflections, and moods of his characters. Melancholy, for example, is experienced by many of his characters. *Mambo Kings* focuses on the inner worlds of the Castillo brothers, Nestor and Cesar, who are both afflicted with an inexplicable melancholy and loneliness. In *Fourteen Sisters*, Emilio is plagued as well by his own solitude and alienation. *Mr. Ives' Christmas* is a religious meditation on the meaning of Christmas and religion in the face of the seemingly pointless death of Mr. Ives's son. *Empress of the Splendid Season* is the story of Lydia Espana, a Cuban cleaning lady, who contemplates love and New York. In *Simple Habana*, Israel Levis, a Cuban composer, returns to Habana after spending time in Paris during the Nazi occupation. While in Paris, Levis is mistaken for a Jew because of his name and is sent to a concentration camp in Buchenwald. He returns to Cuba in 1947 a broken man and spends the last years of his life remembering his one true love. In other words, if asked to describe the novels, the reader would most likely refer to the characters' inner conflict regarding universal themes such as loneliness, alienation, love, and redemption.

Moreover, although the characters have Latin backgrounds, that is not the driving force of this loneliness, but rather a part of each of their characters. Hijuelos himself has said, "I myself often feel extremely lonely. I mean, it's the nature of my work, solitude" (Bowman 1). Man's alienation from himself seems to preoccupy the characters. In this sense, Hijuelos's work addresses universal questions: What is my place on earth? What is my role in this world? His characters are plagued by these profound questions. In fact, in *Mambo Kings,* the immigrant experience is relatively passed over, and Nestor and Cesar Castillo, the two brothers arrive in the United States without pondering their lost homeland or way of life. They quickly find a place to live and a job (thanks to their cousin) and begin to play their music in Manhattan, basically resuming the life they had in Habana. They do not ponder their identity vis-a-vis the bicultural world in which they live. Rather, the two brothers question their anguish, suffering, and pain over and over again. They do not question their bilingual selves (they may not even be bilingual; it is not clear from the novel). The motivating force of their existence is music, and in this music they find release from the solitude that haunts them.

Hijuelos is also obsessed with the Catholic religion, the figure of Christ, and spirituality. This is evident in *Mambo Kings, Mr. Ives' Christmas*, and *A Simple Habana Melody*. Hijuelos asks, "You need to be humble to believe in God, and humility is out of fashion. And yet, you have to ask yourself, with all the horrible tragedy in the world, how can you justify or explain or even think in terms of any kind of God that cares? For me, that goes back to the image of Christ, which is an image of compassion, ultimate compassion, the story of man—the baby in the cradle, the man on the cross, and the resurrection—which is whole" (Harmon 45). The first scene in *Mambo Kings* contains a passage in which Eugenio, Nestor Castillo's son, compares his father's appearance on the *I Love Lucy* show to the resurrection of Christ. Eugenio says, "The miracle had passed, the resurrection of a man, Our Lord's promise which I then believed, with its release from pain, release from the troubles of this world" (*Mambo Kings* 8). In *Mr. Ives' Christmas*, Mr. Ives' faith is tested when his son is randomly killed on the streets of New York. In *Habana Melody*, Israel Levis faces a crisis of faith after experiencing the Holocaust. In the end, Hijuelos's main goal is to render his characters with compassion so that readers will be able to identify with and be moved by the conflicts they experience.

Aside from the complex characters found in Hijuelos's novels, music is the novels' other notable feature. In *Mambo Kings*, Hijuelos details the rise of the *mambo*, a dance with roots in Africa. It became one of the most popular dances in the United States after World War II, which is when the novel takes place. In *A Simple Habana Melody*, Hijuelos focuses on the social dance from which mambo emerged, the *rumba*. Early rumba was created by African slaves, who danced while chained at the feet. As portrayed in his novel, the rumba takes Paris and the United States by storm in the late 1920s and early 1930s. In writing about music in his novels, Hijuelos joins a strong Latin American and, specifically, Cuban group of writers. As scholar William Luis points out, for Hispanics music is considered a link to their homeland; it "reinforces cultural identity and slows or even redefines the immigrant's process of integration" (188). Hijuelos himself is a jazz musician who has performed in some of the nightclubs mentioned in his novel (Luis 190). Hijuelos was born during the mambo craze that swept the United States, specifically Manhattan. He was, however, not old enough to remember the details of that decade, turning nine when the craze was already fading, so he had to rely on research to write his novel. Hijuelos traveled around Manhattan looking for live archives in the form of musicians or their friends who had witnessed the scene. He met some of the famous players, and their friends, who are mentioned in *Mambo Kings*. For instance, he was able to meet Frank Grillo's widow at a local *santera*'s house in Manhattan (Watrous C19). Grillo, better known as Machito, is considered the godfather of Afro-Cuban jazz. He was born in Cuba at the turn of the century. Aside from attempting to meet the greats in Cuban music, Hijuelos also spent time researching the origins of the mambo and the rumba. His novels, in this respect, resemble musical treatises, reflecting the rich and detail-orientated research of a musicologist. Hijuelos emphasizes the power of music brought to the United States by Cubans and reveals how it influenced North American music, especially African American jazz.

The music in Hijuelos's novels provides an historical context and also serves another significant purpose. Music is the life force for the main characters of *Mambo Kings* and *A Simple Habana Melody*. As shall be seen, music transcends grief and allows for healing and the possibility of love. In *Mambo Kings*, Cesar and Nestor cannot live without music, as for them, music equals love and release from pain and grief. In addition, music serves as a narrator of sorts, as the main characters' memories are prompted by the songs they hear. For example, Cesar listens to an old Mambo Kings recording in the Hotel Splendour, where each song reminds him of a different period in his life.

The Mambo Kings Play Songs of Love (1989)

The Mambo Kings Play Songs of Love is divided into five sections. The novel opens and closes with sections narrated by Eugenio Castillo, Nestor's son and Cesar's nephew. In between Eugenio's prologue and epilogue are three sections, all of which take place in 1980 in the Hotel Splendor, a favorite haunt of Cesar Castillo. The three middle sections record Cesar's memories as he commits suicide, literally drinking himself to death while listening to old recordings from his past band, the Mambo Kings. The three middle parts are narrated in the third person singular, but there are moments of a first person singular and footnotes with historical references. Hijuelos does not make it definitive, but because Eugenio's narrative marks the beginning and end of the novel, it seems that Cesar's memories come to us through Eugenio. Another narrative device that Hijuelos uses is music. The three middle sections of Cesar's last memories are prompted by the music he plays. His memories seem to follow the rhythm of the music and take the reader back and forth between past and present. Cesar's memories, recorded on Side A of the novel, begin with his and Nestor's arrival in New York, and end in 1957 with Nestor's death. Side B travels back and forth in time from the years after Nestor's death to their early childhood in the Oriente province of Cuba. The novel recounts not only the rise and fall of a promising mambo group, but also the mambo craze that swept through the country in the 1950s.

The first half of Cesar's memories are found on Side A, "In the Hotel Splendor 1980." This half of the novel follows a chronological order from 1949 to 1960 and records the rise and fall of the Castillo brothers. The action of the novel begins in 1980, as Cesar, at the age of sixty-two, arrives at the Hotel Splendour to kill himself. With a case of whiskey and a stack of old records, he plans to die in the hotel room with alcohol and his memories, which form the core of the novel. This section describes how close the brothers were, their passion for music, as well as the way in which they were opposites. Nestor was the quiet, melancholic brother, obsessed with a woman he had left behind in Cuba who becomes the inspiration for the song that makes them famous, "Beautiful María of My Soul." Although the song is immediately popular, Nestor rewrites it twenty-two times, seeking to capture his lost love. Cesar is portrayed as the complete opposite, carefree and, after a brief marriage in Cuba, not faithful to any woman. Cesar finds satisfaction in a multitude of relationships. This part also records the apex of the brothers' success, their appearance on the *I Love Lucy* show in 1955, and the success of the song "Beautiful María of My Soul." It also contains the marriage of Delores and Nestor and a multitude of Cesar's relationships, with special attention paid to Vanna Vane. This part ends with Cesar's abrupt downfall when he gives up on playing music because it reminds him too much of his brother Nestor.

After Nestor's death in a car accident, Cesar decides to give up on music and take a job as a superintendent in his building. The second part, Side B, "Sometime Later in the Night in the Hotel Splendour" is nonlinear in structure, moving back and forth between past and present. The ambiguity of narrative perspective aids in the creation of "scrambled egg" memories, the drunken memories of Cesar's last night on earth. It describes in detail the life of the Castillo brothers in Oriente, Cuba, as a poor struggling family. It also highlights Cesar's discovery, as a child in Cuba, of the power of music, one of the most important scenes in the novel. Despite their obvious differences, the brothers are actually two sides of the same coin. In the end, Cesar becomes, in many ways, Nestor.

One of the most significant memories, and one that Cesar will keep revisiting, is that of his first music lesson. One day he hears a musician named Eusebio Stevenson playing in Cuba. He follows Eusebio Stevenson, begging him for music lessons. Cesar promises the teacher food and rum in exchange for lessons. His desire to be taught is so great that it is one of the few times that he cries. Stevenson finally agrees to teach Cesar if the child brings rum. When Cesar's father discovers this, he beats Cesar. What Cesar does for music is incomprehensible to his father. Cesar recalls this beating, the worst of all of them, as what damaged their relationship: "And he remembers how that really started all the bad blood between him and his father, because now his son was not only a free spirit but a thief to boot!" (*Mambo Kings* 385). His love of music is then forever linked to the beatings he received from his father. Initially, learning music is a transgressive act. At the same time, his teacher gives him his greatest lesson; he tells Cesar that when playing music, you must communicate love. Love is music; love is beautiful. So Cesar links music with love, even though grief surrounds him everywhere. His last memories will be dictated by what the music tells him, "Yes, love was so beautiful, the music told him, taking him again to his friends" (*Mambo Kings* 389). With the music as a guide, Cesar will say *adiós* to his childhood friends. Without music, Cesar's soul withers. After Nestor's death, Cesar was changed and abandoned music: "He lost his feeling for music and his soul withered" (*Mambo Kings* 202).

In fact, this memory, or engraving of music, and how it provides love links Side B to the section "Towards the End." In this section, Cesar remembers all of the women he has loved and how each one of them gave him a gift. But, above all, he recalls his mother and the power of maternal love as the most important gift on earth. His mother is linked with the stars, "with the morning light, the light burning through the treetops" (*Mambo Kings* 387). In the end, the Cesar portrayed throughout the novel, the reckless and sexually obsessive Cesar, actually was loved and loved. After Nestor's death, Cesar becomes more and more like Nestor. In the final section of Cesar's memories, he even rewrites Nestor's song, "Beautiful María," which links him forever to Nestor's obsessive and melancholy nature. Nestor and Cesar can be described as two sides of the same coin. When Nestor dies, Cesar continues Nestor's suffering as a martyr. He indulges in his sexual binges, always seeking release from his pain. In the end, in fact in the section titled "Towards the End," as the song relentlessly brings Cesar nearer death, we realize that he has become what Nestor always was, that he sits in his armchair "brooding constantly like a ruined poet or an old man" (*Mambo Kings* 137). In fact, Cesar has consciously adopted Nestor's personality in order to suffer for redemption.

Eugenio's prologue and epilogue record his long-lasting memory of the appearance of his father and uncle on the *I Love Lucy* show, singing their famous song "Beautiful María of My Soul." Their appearance on the show, which Eugenio characterizes as "an item of eternity" (*Mambo Kings* 3), shows him not only his father but also a certain time period, the mambo craze, immortalized. The epilogue recounts his trip to Los Angeles, where he meets Desi Arnaz, an icon in Cuban American pop culture, who has also vanished from the public imagination and stands as a relic of a time long past.

CULTURAL ELEMENTS

The Mambo Kings Play Songs of Love, originally titled *The Secrets of a Poor Man*, is one of the first novels to be recognized as the new Cuban American literature, as critic Bruce-Novoa points out. Yet, although it shares some common themes with previous Latino immigrant novels—the Castillo brothers arrive in New York in order to make their fortune, work hard, and reach some sort of stability—the similarities end there since the novel does not focus on the immigrant struggle. In fact, Hijuelos's novel did not receive much attention from other Cuban Americans or from critics of Latino literature (Pérez Firmat *Life on the Hyphen* 137) because it failed to concern itself with the exile of those immigrants from the Castro Revolution and it did not "pledge allegiance to its Cuban roots" (Pérez Firmat "I Came, I Saw, I Conga'd" 241). Instead, it focused on the inner world of the characters. This idea, that Latino literature need not obsess on the nature of ethnicity and the lost homeland, is, in fact, Hijuelos's contribution to Latino literature.

Although *Mambo Kings* lends itself to the typical "immigrant story" interpretation (Luis 196), it goes well beyond this framework as well. Hijuelos himself has stated that *Mambo Kings* is not an immigrant novel (Waltrous C17) because the characters focus on music and on each other. Nestor would suffer the loss of María no matter where he lived, Cuba or the United States. Cesar would end up a lonely man in either geographical location. In this respect, the loss of a homeland is not the root of the characters' problems, but rather part of the larger universal questions that concern Hijuelos as a writer. The characters are not in search of a balanced identity in their new homeland; they are in search of a balanced identity because of a lost love or loneliness. Unlike many of the characters included here, Cesar and Nestor Castillo are not seeking to assimilate or to find a balanced identity between their Cuban and adoptive country. They remain Cuban throughout the novel, they are probably speaking Spanish throughout the novel, and they are obsessed with the idea of the macho Cuban. The Castillo brothers want to belong to the music scene, more than anything else. Cesar and Nestor come to the United States to continue their musical careers, and their arrival in New York does not change that dream.

The lack of musical opportunities drive Cesar and Nestor to New York. The Cuba that Nestor and Cesar leave behind is the Cuba "for the prosperous British and Americans," who traveled there for their vacations, for release from the stringent days of World War II. The Castillo brothers leave ten years before Castro comes to power, during Prío Socarás's brief reign. At the time, Cuba was the playground for other nations, for tourists. But, the real reason the brothers leave is the introduction of movies with sound. This, as the novel points out, led to a lack of employment for theater orchestras, and many musicians sought jobs both in Habana and beyond. Side A captures the fast-paced and rich musical scene that thrived in New York during the fifties as more and more Cubans came to this musical hub. Side A, in this respect, is a frenzy, a mambo song that begins with the brothers' ascent to brief fame, in 1955, and then a rapid fall. The novel dramatically captures the historical wave of music that swept through New York between 1949–1956. Hijuelos repeatedly alludes to the popularity of Latin music with long paragraphs that list the records, musicians, clubs, and songs that characterized the era. In this sense, the novel functions as an historical novel; it includes dates and footnotes of historical accuracy. Although the popularity of the mambo and its recordings had practically vanished by the 1970s, the Cuban rhythms have had a lasting impact on North American culture. In fact, the novel reverses the North American cultural influence on Latinos and its resulting effects by emphasizing the Cuban musical influence on North American culture. Hijuelos includes small (invented or not) details, like the logo for Chesterfield cigarettes, that indicate the impact musicians like the Mambo Kings and the mambo itself had on North Americans: "Folks, smoke Chesterfields, the preferred tobacco, the Mambo Kings' favorite" (*Mambo Kings* 12).

The Revolution is mentioned in Side B, but it does not take center stage, nor does it truly affect the brothers in any significant way. Although Cesar does comment at one point that he would return to Cuba if it weren't for the revolution, and although he does return to music to send money to his brothers, who eventually migrate to Miami, the revolution does not obsess Cesar. In fact, when his brothers write to tell him of their difficulties under Castro, Cesar does not politicize, but rather sees it as a way to redeem himself after having lost his brother Nestor.

The novel points to a specific time in history, when Latin culture influenced North American Culture. There are two defining cultural elements in this novel: The *I Love Lucy Show* on television and "Beautiful María of My Soul," the song that is played over and over again on the radio and in clubs. Both serve as cultural markers for Cuban male identity. As Gustavo Pérez-Firmat has remarked, both Cubans and North Americans "acquired many notions of how Cubans behave, talk, lose their temper, and treat or mistreat their wives by watching Ricky love Lucy" (2). The other side of the story, however, is that portrayed by Hijuelos. Desi Arnaz was indeed a Cuban male model to which many aspired. He was not a model because he was comical and assimilated, or because he spoke Spanish a mile a minute, as was comically portrayed on the television show. He was revered for his legitimate musical talents and the historical quality that characterized his presence in the United States before he became a household name. Desi Arnaz, as Pérez-Firmat points out, was the person who first led a conga dance on the mainland in 1937, twelve years before the Mambo Kings in Hijuelos's novel arrived in New York (2).

Cesar's music is linked to his machismo and his sexuality. One important theme discussed in this book, seen only in passing in the other novels, is that of the *macho*. Machismo literally means an exaggerated show of masculinity, a show of male chauvinism. A macho is a pretentiously manly or virile man.

Hijuelos concerns himself with this theme in his autobiographical novel *Our House,* and it appears center stage in *Mambo Kings* as well. Cesar and Nestor are preoccupied with the Cuban macho self and how to live up to it. Cesar is a hard-drinking womanizer whom no woman can keep. He literally struts around Manhattan until his very death. His exterior self displays all the macho qualities that are expected of the Latino male. Yet, Hijuelos's gift to his characters is to note their interior struggle with this very macho self. In the end, what Cesar misses most is the affection and care of his mother, the simple bath that his mother used to give him as a child. In this sense, the novel expresses a yearning for a lost identity, not so much a lost homeland. Whatever sensitivity the brothers harbored as children was beaten out of them by their father. In addition, the final memory—of the mother caring for her child—forces the reader to question the female role in creating the macho man. Are Cesar's final memories of his mother that of a macho who adores the mother and places her on a pedestal, while acting misogynistically toward other women?

Cesar, remembers how the definition of macho is formed: "No softness in Pedro's face, no kindness, no compassion. Pedro was a real man. He worked hard, had his women on the side, showed his strength to his sons. His manliness was such that it permeated the household with a scent of meat, tobacco, and homemade rum" (*Mambo Kings* 214). Yet, the mother tells her badly abused and beaten sons that their father has "a heart of gold" (*Mambo Kings* 214). Nestor is the more introspective of the two. When he meets the woman of his dreams, he confesses all his lifelong insecurities and fears about not being a real man.

Finally, another important aspect of Cuban American life that is examined in the novel is the sense of community that characterized the Cuban immigrants. It was a time, the narrator says, when every Cuban knew every other Cuban. This sense of community, especially among musicians, is portrayed throughout the novel, as members of the community aid each other in securing jobs, and share food, dance, and memories. The extended Cuban community in New York is shown to be a close-knit one in the beginning of the novel. It is a pre-Castro, pre-Golden Exile age when not many Cubans were in New York. Between 1960 and 1995 more than 1 million Cubans arrived in the United States. The first wave of immigrants who left because of Castro were called the Golden Exiles because they were doctors, lawyers, professors, and other types of professionals. But, Cesar and Nestor predate the Cuban revolution.

Section one provides an historical description of how the band was formed and reminisces about the excitement of being in New York among so many musicians. It speaks briefly to the racial hierarchy that prevailed in the United States: One flyer says, "No zoot suits and no jitterbugs," which means no Mexicans or Blacks, who remained at the bottom of the social ladder, were allowed (*Mambo Kings* 29). Cesar and Nestor, however, are light-skinned Cubans like Desi Arnaz, thus allowed in most clubs. The fame of the Castillo brothers comes at a time when Latin music is the vogue. Musicians like Tito Puente are the rage, and the rumba and the chachacha have broken onto the scene. It is a time when 78 RMP records are ten cents apiece. Hijuelos captures a time long gone in Cuba as well. And, as Cesar's memories become increasingly disparate, he remembers his home, Cuba, along with his mother, as an idyllic past. Cesar's memories of Cuba and New York in the fifties contrast with the present, 1980. For example, at the time of his arrival and in the fifties, people treated one another with respect, there was less crime, and there was a stronger sense of community. When the novel ends, Cesar describes a much more violent New York, where to travel on the subway alone is to risk your life.

The neighborhood, or La Salle Street, and the Hotel Splendour are the two geographical focal points in the novel. By the end of the novel, left with his memories, Cesar recalls that most of the great musicians he knew have vanished. There was a time when most Cubans knew each other and knew all of the musicians, but now, in the 1980s, most musicians are dead. Cesar's death, in this respect, formally ends the mambo era.

FURTHER SUGGESTED READINGS

Works by Oscar Hijuelos

Hijuelos, Oscar. *A Simple Habana Melody (from when times were good)*. New York: HarperCollins, 2002.

———. *Empress of the Splendid Season*. New York: HarperCollins, 1999.

———. *Mr. Ives' Christmas*. New York: Perennial, 1996.

———. *The Fourteen Sisters of Emilio Montez O'Brien*. New York: Harper Perennial Paperbacks, 1993.

———. *The Mambo Kings Play Songs of Love: A Novel*. New York: HarperCollins, 1990.

———. *Our House in the Last World*. New York: Persea Books, 1989.

Other Suggested Readings

Bowman, David. "The Empress of the Splendid Season: The Barnes and Noble Review" <http://www.barnesandnoble.com_theempressofthesplendidseason>, June 20, 2003.

Bruce-Novoa, Juan. "Hijuelos' *Mambo Kings*: Reading from Divergent Traditions." *Confluencia* 10:2 (Spring 1995) 11-22.

Harmon, A.G. "A Conversation with Oscar Hijuelos." *Image: A Journal of Arts and Religion* 22 (Winter–Spring 1999) 43-57.

Muñoz, Elias Miguel. *Brand New Memory*. Houston: Arte Público Press, 1998.

Pau Llosa, Ricardo. *Sorting Metaphors*. Tallahassee: Anhinga Press, 1983.

Pérez-Firmat, Gustavo. *Anything but Love*. Houston: Arte Público Press, 2000.

————. "I Came, I Saw, I Conga'd: Contexts for a Cuban American Culture." Delgado and Muñoz, Eds. *Everynight Life: Culture and Dance in Latino America*. Durham, NC: Duke University Press, 1997.

————. *Life on the Hyphen: The Cuban-American Way*. Austin: University of Texas Press, 1994.

Suarez, Virgil. *Havana Thursdays*. Houston: Arte Público Press, 1995.

Waltrous, Peter. "Evoking When Mambo was King." *The New York Times*. Monday, September 11, 1989.

Chapter 7
The Fiction of Judith Ortiz Cofer: The Line of the Sun *(1989)*

Judith Ortiz Cofer was born in the western town of Hormigueros, Puerto Rico, in 1952. When her father joined the navy, the family moved to Brooklyn, New York. In 1955, they moved to Paterson, New Jersey, where the early years of Ortiz Cofer's childhood were spent. Whenever her father was away on long trips, Ortiz Cofer's mother would return with her children to Puerto Rico. What most influenced Ortiz Cofer on these frequent returns to the tropical island were the stories she heard. While braiding her granddaughters' hair, Ortiz Cofer's grandmother would tell stories about the family and the traditions and myths of Puerto Rico (Ortiz Cofer *Silent Dancing* 14–15). Depending on her audience and the moral lesson she wanted to convey, Ortiz Cofer's grandmother would tell the same story differently each time. Storytelling, Ortiz Cofer discovered, is not only for entertainment, but to preserve cultural memories and to teach lessons: "I give credit to the women in my family for giving me this lesson and some of the original stories that I used" (Kevane and Heredia 116). In her work, Ortiz Cofer continually calls upon the craft of telling stories through the matriarchal line—mothers, grandmothers, and daughters gathered in the domestic spaces of the home, the kitchen, or the porch to tell, to listen, and to learn from a storyteller. Although *los cuentos*, oral stories, form the backbone of her poetry, essays, and novel, what ultimately matters in storytelling, Ortiz Cofer learned from her grandmother, is the poetic truth. Ortiz Cofer describes the poetic truth as the attempt to communicate the emotional substance of a story rather than the exact photographic memory of it (Kevane and Heredia 116). Aside from the importance of poetic truth, factual historical truth, especially with regard to Puerto Rican history, is a concern as well. Ortiz Cofer never publishes a novel or poem about Puerto Rico without consulting her friends who are historians and literary critics. Her obsession derives from her sense of responsibility and obligation to both North American and Puerto Rican readers. Her novel might be the only literature that someone reads about Puerto Rico. Ortiz Cofer wants her readers to have the correct information about this tiny Caribbean island.

In 1968, upon her father's retirement from the navy, Ortiz Cofer's family finally settled in Augusta, Georgia, where she attended high school and college. Ortiz Cofer later received her M.A. in English from Florida Atlantic University. She lives in Athens, Georgia, where she has been an English professor at the University of Georgia for more than twenty years, and where she currently holds the Franklin Chair in English. Although she did not grow up in a Latino community, like the "Nuyorican" community that characterizes Puerto Ricans in New York, she "never abandoned the island of my birth, or perhaps that obsession called 'the island' never left me" ("Latina Writer?" 11). Ortiz Cofer's first books were collections of poetry, *Peregrina* (1986), *Terms of Survival* (1987) and *Reaching for the Mainland* (1987). In 1989 she published her first novel, *The Line of the Sun*, and a year later *Silent Dancing: A Partial Remembrance of a Puerto Rican Childhood*, which incorporates essays and poetry to describe her early childhood. In 1995, she published *The Latin Deli*, and later a young adult's book and a collection of essays, *Woman in Front of the Sun* (2001). For Ortiz Cofer, writing functions "as a bridge, so that, unlike my parents, I would not be precariously straddling the cultures, always fearing the fall, anxious as to which side they really belonged; I would be crossing the bridge of my design and construction, at will; not abandoning either side, but traveling back and forth without fear and confusion as to where I belonged—I belong to both" ("Latina Writer?" 13). This autobiographical concern is rendered fictionally in her novel *The Line of the Sun*. Marisol, the narrator of the novel, who serves as Ortiz Cofer's alter ego, also strives to write in order to understand a life caught between two cultures (*The Line* 290). The novel contains a fair deal of autobiographical material in terms of other characters as well: the characters Guzmán, Rafael, and Ramona, for instance, are based on Ortiz Cofer's uncle and parents. Her uncle, like Guzmán, was the black sheep of her mother's family; her father, like Rafael, was in the navy, and her mother, like Ramona, had a difficult time assimilating. Autobiographical links between the novel and Ortiz Cofer's life can be found not only in *A Partial Remembrance*, but also in several essays found in *Woman in Front of the Sun*.

The Line of the Sun (1989)

The Line of the Sun contains twelve chapters that can be divided into two parts. The first part, which includes Chapters 1–6, takes place on the island, in a rural setting in the town of Salud, based, Ortiz Cofer says, on her hometown. Chapters 7–12, comprising the second part, takes place on the mainland, in a vertical *barrio*, an island-tower called *El Building*, in Paterson, New Jersey. Part I narrates Guzmán's adventures in Puerto Rico, whereas Part II narrates his adventures in New Jersey, and specifically in *El Building*. The epilogue stands outside of the time frame of the novel and serves as a kind of literary manifesto, or a statement by the narrator, Marisol, revealing how she became a writer. In this sense the novel is reminiscent of many already studied in this book. The narrator becomes the writer in order to understand her bicultural and bilingual heritage. (Yolanda in *García Girls*, Pilar in *Dreaming in Cuban*, Esperanza in *The House on Mango Street*, all become writers for this reason.) Just as the novel is divided between two geographical sites, it is also divided into two family struggles, each of which revolve around or are caused by the character Guzmán.

The theme of the novel in the first half is survival within the strictures of the small religious and morally upright *pueblo* of Salud whereas, in the second half, it is survival in America. Guzmán, who acts as a satellite around which the other characters revolve, appears in both halves and drives the action and conflict of both parts. Resolutions occur as well because Guzmán creates conflict and forces the characters to face issues that they otherwise might not. In the epilogue we realize that Ramona was not able to face life in the United States and thus returns home. The narrator Marisol, on the other hand, inspired by her experiences with her uncle Guzmán, has discovered how to survive through telling stories and through writing.

Chapters 1 through 5 narrate "Guzmán's Adventures," as Marisol later describes them, in the small rural town of Salud. Guzmán Vivente, characterized as the *niño del diablo* (devil's child) and the wild child from the moment he is born, tests the standards of the Catholic and morally upright town of Salud. According to a legend, Salud is the result of a miracle; the Virgin cured the wound of a woodcutter who was gored by a bull by saying "salud," which means health. The legend says that the woodcutter and bull bowed to their knees in front of the Virgin. For many years, Puerto Ricans from around the island would visit this spot and pray to the Shrine of Our Lady of Salud, hoping for a cure for some illness or for a better life. Finally, the Catholic Church decided to build a cathedral in honor of *La Virgen*. With the help of the Taino Indians, the native Indians of the island who were decimated by the Spaniards, a church named Nuestra Señora de la Salud was erected on a hilltop overlooking the town of Salud: "And so Salud grew around the church, the little houses built to face the Holy Hill, where it sits like a great white hen spreading her marble wings over the town" (*Line of the Sun* 46). This "great white hen" reminds the people of Salud of their sins and of their duties to the church.

The Vivente and Santacruz families, whose lives intersect because of Guzmán, live in this small town. Guzmán, the wild, second-oldest son of Mamá Cielo and Papá Pepe, causes so much conflict that Mamá Cielo (at the suggestion of the nosy neighbor Doña Julia) decides to take her problematic son to Rosa, *La Cabra*, the town *spiritist* and whore. Rosa lives outside of this small town and, therefore, outside of its strictures as well. Rosa, *La Cabra*, who is viewed as evil but also receives visits from everyone in the town, convinces Mamá Cielo during the *despojo* (exorcism), to leave Guzmán with her. Guzmán soon falls in love with Rosa and, at the age of fifteen, he moves in with her. In Rosa's home, located in an idealized valley that stands outside of Salud, Guzmán learns about real love and freedom. He receives a "sentimental education" that he will never forget, an education that keeps him on the outside forever. He learns about pure love, freedom, the natural world, plants and their cures, and the beauty of nature. In addition, he learns English, as Rosa has a television that only carries North American channels. This will serve him well in New York a couple of years later.

Although Guzmán and Rosa are happy in the idyllic world they share outside the moral and geographical boundaries of Salud, Mamá Cielo is scandalized and wants her son back. She does not like that he has a shameful lifestyle and lives in sin. The Holy Rosary Society, made up of a group of women who take it upon themselves to guard "the moral status of the town" (*Line of the Sun* 76), decide to rescue Guzmán from the evil woman. This rescue is, according to Marisol, the last witch-hunt that the town of Salud would endure. The witch-hunt is described by Ortiz Cofer with a great deal of humor that includes sharp criticism of the Catholic Church and of those who espouse the church's morality. Rosa is driven from Salud forever and forces Guzmán's eventual departure as well.

For a while, Guzmán retreats completely from Salud; he lives in hiding and on the fringes of society until *la lotería* comes to town. The lottery, begun during President Truman's administration, promised the young men of Puerto Rico economic employment and better opportunities on the mainland. Guzmán participates in this opportunity, even though we learn later that it is a form of abuse and exploitation. With Guzmán's departure, the narration quickly sums up the marriage of Ramona and Rafael Vivente, who had become Guzmán's best friends, and their impending move to the Untied States. Rafael, who admires the United States, firmly believes that life will be better on the mainland. Ramona, on the other hand, already indicates that she will not assimilate to America, "I will never learn English, Rafael" (*Line of the Sun* 167). It also relates the birth of the narrator, Marisol, who is not only born in Mamá Cielo's house but who, like Guzmán, is the product of a difficult birth: "Because of the slow fingers of an old midwife I nearly bled to death on my first day on earth. Mamá Cielo's vigils and her herbal teas kept my mother strong, and Ramona's warm body and plentiful milk convinced me I should stay" (*Line of the Sun* 168).

The second part begins with Chapter 7 and life in *El Building*, a vertical *barrio* of Puerto Ricans in Paterson, New Jersey. The chapter ends with the arrival of the mysterious Guzmán, of whom Marisol and her brother Gabriel have heard countless stories, and with the arrival of Marisol's menstruation, a definite mark of her changing body and identity. Mamá Cielo and Papá Pepe's home, the rural town of Salud, and the gossip and struggles that characterize Salud, are now juxtaposed with those found in the United States. Rafael, although rarely present, leaves his mark on the family. He expects his children to be well educated, to study hard, and to assimilate to their new life. He hopes to convince Ramona to leave *El Building*, which he does not perceive as safe or respectable. Ramona, on the other hand, is not acculturated, speaks no English, is afraid to leave the environment of *El Building*, and successfully creates an island within her own apartment. Marisol is thirteen and is suffering in the bilingual and bicultural world which she now inhabits: "At thirteen, I was being counseled in humble acceptance of a destiny I had not chosen for myself: exile or, worse, homelessness. I was already very much aware of the fact that I fit into neither the white middle-class world of my classmates at Saint Jerome's nor the exclusive club of El Building's 'expatriates'"(*Line of the Sun* 177).

Marisol now takes center stage, and we follow her life from the age of thirteen to fifteen, and then again, as an adult, in the epilogue. Marisol describes the Puerto Rican community in Paterson, New Jersey, with her mother Ramona, her absent father, and Gabriel, her brother. Guzmán's arrival causes immediate excitement and a change within the family. When Guzmán is injured by a local tenant, Marisol slowly gravitates toward Guzmán, becoming his caretaker and an audience for his stories. Marisol's fascination with Guzmán coincides with her rebellious adolescence. She becomes attached to Guzmán as a way out of the strict rules that apply in her home. Her mother does not give her any freedom even though, as Marisol states, at her age her mother, Ramona, was already married: "I was almost fifteen now—still in my silly uniform, bobby socks and all; still not allowed to socialize with my friends, living in a state of limbo, halfway between cultures" (*Line of the Sun* 222). In her isolation, with her competing cultural traditions, Marisol focuses more and more on Guzmán.

Aside from Marisol's growing attachment to Guzmán, the action of this half of the novel also centers on the women's attention to a *spiritist* meeting they are planning. The planning of the meeting allows the women the ability to meet with each other and create a sense of purpose and belonging denied them outside of *El Building*. Parallel to their preparation for the big *spiritist* meeting, the men are preparing a *huelga* (strike) against the factories that employ them. As in other fiction, the struggle for employment by Latino men remains a source of conflict. The Puerto Ricans are treated as third-class citizens, overworked and abused. The second half of the novel is resolved when a fire breaks out at the *spiritist* meeting, burning down the building and forcing Rafael's family to move to the suburbs. The epilogue, narrated by Marisol as an adult, reflects on the family's move to the suburbs,

Rafael's death, Ramona's return to the island, and Marisol's beginnings as a writer. Marisol has, in effect, become the bridge that Ortiz Cofer spoke of, the bridge that allows her to cross back and forth "without fear and confusion."

CULTURAL ELEMENTS

The Line of the Sun narrates the story of Puerto Ricans on the island and of Puerto Ricans in New Jersey. The action of the novel takes place between the late 1940s and the early 1960s, and it is neatly divided between life in Salud and life in Paterson, New Jersey, specifically in *El Building*. Several historical events are described within this time period that are directly related to Puerto Rico's economic and social transformation and the subsequent migration of Puerto Ricans to the United States. Ortiz Cofer portrays how the economic changes affect both the Vivente (Mamá Cielo, Papá Pepe, Carmelo, Guzmán, Ramona, and Luz) and the Santacruz families (Rafael and his father) while they are living on the island.

The most important change during this time was Operation Bootstrap, the economic agreement reached between Puerto Rico's first elected governor, Luis Muñoz Marín, and President Harry S Truman in 1947. Termed an "economic miracle," it transformed Puerto Rico's poverty-stricken rural economy into a highly successful industrial one. The pact was meant to be mutually beneficial; companies in the United States were granted tax exemptions if they took their manufacturing businesses to the island, and Puerto Ricans would be employed in them, which would ease the high unemployment rate on the island. With the opening of United States-owned industries, Puerto Rico's economy would become modernized. But, the transformation also produced the "great migration." Even though United States-based companies opened many factories on the island, as the agricultural economy was phased out and urbanized, thousands were left unemployed. In response to this unemployment, part of the Operation Bootstrap agreement was to offer Puerto Ricans jobs on the mainland. During the 1950s, almost 500,000 Puerto Ricans emigrated to the United States. Guzmán and Rafael are participants in this emigration for different reasons, although both share the belief that life will improve on the mainland and that they will find better employment and opportunities. The exodus was so great that it became typical for families throughout the island to have at least one member of their family or their community in the United States.

The industrialization of the island and the phasing out of agricultural economies directly affects the Vivente family, who have been dependent on the sugar-cane plantation and the refinery called the "*Central.*" Mamá Cielo and her two sons make and sell lunch to the sugar-cane workers to supplement their income. The Santacruz family, Rafael and his father, work on the sugar-cane plantation owned by the one American who appears in the novel, Mr. Clement. Rafael works as a cutter, and his father is the *mayordomo* (overseer) of the plantation. Mr. Clement lives in the "Big House," a house with plumbing and electricity that stands above the plantation—as the church does above the town—and that symbolizes the ever-growing American presence and its control over the local economy.

The Korean War is another major event that is addressed in the novel. It was the second war in which Puerto Ricans, as United States citizens, actively served. Carmelo, the oldest son of the Vivente family, like many other Puerto Ricans, dies in this war. The 65th Infantry Regiment or "The Borinqueneers," as the Puerto Rican contingency was know, proved to be a key element in the war. There were individual feats of heroism, as well as collective efforts to support the United States in this war. The troops, however, suffered many casualties: "One out of every 42 casualties was a Puerto Rican; and the island had one casualty for every 660 inhabitants, compared to one casualty for every 1,125 inhabitants of the United States" (Morales Carrión 286). Because of unemployment on the island, many Puerto Rican soldiers who had actively served the United States, came to the mainland in the hopes of being accepted for their wartime efforts and, thereby, of finding opportunities.

The culture of emigration from island to mainland depended on the idea of return (with a romanticized and idealized notion of the island), and on the hopes of recreating the homeland on the mainland. Most Puerto Ricans thought they would arrive in the United States, work hard for a couple of years, and then return home and buy a little *finca* (farm) where they would retire. However, for most Puerto Ricans who left the island, illusions about how life would improve in the United States were typically met with disappointment. First, although the trip to New York was never thought of as permanent, it usually became permanent. Few were able to return, as they were caught in a vicious cycle of economic hardship. Upon arriving on the mainland, Puerto Ricans, although American citizens, were treated as third-class citizens and confronted racism and destructive stereotypes. Whether heroes of the Korean War, laborers like Guzmán, or citizens searching for economic opportunities, most Puerto Ricans faced a grim reality. Workers like Guzmán were exploited and abused, most were discriminated against and treated as outsiders. Puerto Ricans today continue to fight poverty, unemployment, drug use, crime, and a high rate of school dropouts. Stereotypes persist to this day about Puerto Ricans: that they are the Latino welfare population, that they have failed to succeed in the United States, that they are drug addicts, and more. Despite the fact that the mainland did not fulfill the dreams of many Puerto Ricans, Puerto Ricans continued to emigrate to the mainland. Today, Puerto Rico is characterized as a nation in constant travel on the *guagua aérea*, the air bus, as Puerto Rican writer Luis Rafael Sánchez called it, traveling back and forth between the mainland and the island. In Ortiz Cofer's novel, the characters are constantly moving back and forth between island and mainland.

Once on the mainland, many Puerto Ricans gravitated toward each other. In Ortiz Cofer's novel, it is to a building in Paterson, New Jersey, where they can settle, search for employment, and enjoy a support network. *El Building*, the vertical *barrio*, is the focal point for the Santacruz family and for Guzmán in the United States. Ortiz Cofer portrays ordinary Puerto Ricans who do not belong to gangs, who are not dying of hunger, and who are not addicted to drugs. They are poor, but they have *orgullo* (pride) and a sense of responsibility. They face *la lucha* (the daily struggle) with dignity as they attempt to create a new future and a better life for their children. One way to offset the daily struggle is to recreate the homeland on the mainland. The obsessive need to duplicate island culture on the mainland functions as a strategy of survival, a way of dealing with the inability to assimilate to American culture, or as a way to avoid assimilation. On the verge of their departure to the United States, Ramona tells Rafael that she will not learn English. Indeed, she does not. She has no need to learn the ways of the dominant culture because in *El Building* she is among other Puerto Ricans, and also because Marisol becomes her interpreter. In fact, not until the end of the novel does Ramona make any adjustments or contact with the dominant culture, and then only because she has moved out of *El Building*. The building is described frequently as its own microcosm of Puerto Ricans, where life is lived at a "high pitch" (172) and the women in the family attempt to recreate island culture within the confines of their apartments.

Although within the community of *El Building* Puerto Ricans feel safe, outside of that insular world, it is a different story. Marisol refers to *la mancha* (the stain), or the "sign of the wetback," and the frightened look of the foreigners, as well as further indicators of otherness. Marisol is well aware of her differences and those of her mother. She describes how her schoolmates stare at her mother, Ramona, because of her clothes, the colors she wears, her makeup, and the way she walks. To the Anglo American culture in New Jersey, it is clear that Ramona is from another country. Although Marisol's mother refuses to adapt to the dominant culture, and eventually returns to Puerto Rico, the rest of the family feels differently. Marisol and Gabriel, her younger brother, wish their mother would make an attempt to belong. In fact, when they move, Gabriel, a reclusive bookworm, grows more confident as he adjusts to the quieter life of the suburbs and feels more at home than he ever did in *El Building*. Marisol also notes that she is not truly a part of *El Building*, nor is she part of the dominant culture. Unlike the other kids in *El Building*, Marisol studies at a private school. In addition, she notes that her family is economically stable and does not fit into the socioeconomic class of the other families. At the same time, she does not fit into the environment of her private school; she knows, as do the other students, that she is different because she is not Anglo American. Also, unlike her peers who live in the suburbs, Marisol lives in *El Building*, which marks her as radically different. Marisol is embarrassed by the noise, the food, and the activity of her home and environment. Rafael also feels alienated from the Puerto Rican community in Paterson not only because he is gainfully employed in the Navy and is rarely around, but also because he finds the building a distasteful place and not a fitting one for his family. He discriminates against his own, seeing *El Building* as a dangerous place full of "street-tough Puerto Rican immigrants" who are different from the "the usually gentle and hospitable Islander" (*Line of the Sun* 170).

Idealizing and romanticizing the homeland, the Puerto Rico left behind, is a favorite pastime for Puerto Ricans in Marisol's building. The lament for their lost homeland, to which they cannot return because of their economic situation, is a bond that they all share. Readers, however, must recognize that the longing for Puerto Rico is deceptive; life in Salud was not easy. Ramona, for instance, who pines for Puerto Rico, led a hard-working life there, taking care of her mother's children and working from dawn until night. Most men could not find employment, gossip destroyed people's lives, and Salud itself was nothing more than a dust bowl. But, while living in the United States, Puerto Ricans develop the habit of creating a pure and beautiful home that will be the answer to all of their struggles, just as America was the answer to all of their struggles on the island.

Gender roles are as carefully monitored in *El Building* as they were in Salud. Most men follow the same mores that characterize the island patriarchal system. Men can have affairs; women cannot. Men can come and go as they please; women cannot. Marisol, for example, resents the fact that she is so closely monitored by her parents, that her sexual identity is protected. Her parents do not grant her any freedom, especially when she becomes a *señorita* (a young woman), someone who has begun her menstruation. Rafael thinks Marisol is at risk in the building, especially now that she is a *señorita*: "We have to be careful with her," he says. "Have you seen her with any boys? I don't want her mixing with the hoodlums in this place" (*Line of the Sun* 180). Becoming a *señorita* is not only a rite of passage, but also a dangerous stage during which a girl's virginity must be protected at all costs. The men visit whores but protect their sisters' virginity. Ramona, who married at Marisol's age, fifteen, participates in this because if her daughter were to become pregnant, Ramona would be blamed.

Honor codes exist, as well, regarding gender. For example, men are allowed to compliment women but not touch them: "Respectable wives and their daughters could be looked over and, if unescorted, even verbally complimented. . . . But it was strictly hands off; if that unspoken rule was violated, revenge was usually swift" (*Line of the Sun* 186). In this respect, Marisol and Ramona feel safe even though they are objects of male scrutiny. Despite the gender differences and the separation between men and women, both share a certain sense of frustration. The women are frustrated by the restrictions placed upon them by the men, the domestic abuse, the men's unfaithfulness, the lack of opportunity for them. The men, in turn, are frustrated by the abuse they receive at their jobs, the struggle to make ends meet; and the discrimination they face. Both men and women create places of sanctity. The basement is the men's sacred place, forbidden to women. In the basement the men gamble, drink, smoke, pass the time, talk, and organize their *huelga* (strike) against low wages. The women, in turn, share the domestic space of the kitchen, which is where they plan their *spiritist* meeting.

Although the men keep sharp control over their women, the women are mostly left to their own devices while the husbands work in factories, or seek jobs when they are laid off. The women become empowered through alternative means; the kitchen becomes their center of cultural sharing, of collective sorrows and joys. In the kitchen, their sanctified space, they also empower themselves through *los cuentos*. Stories are a means of survival for Ramona and Marisol; Ramona depends on stories to keep her connected to her past, whereas Marisol depends on them for her future. Conversations at the kitchen table, the center of the domestic female space, become Marisol's stories as a writer. These conversations contain not only gossip and arguments, but the narration of memories that are meant to endure and inspire. Marisol, like Ortiz Cofer, will depend on these stories to get her through *la lucha* (the daily struggle). She hears the stories between Guzmán and Rafael, between Guzmán and Ramona, between her parents, and between the women. The kitchen table is the center from which Marisol is able to create history, a past for herself.

The title, *The Line of the Sun*, refers to *espiritismo* (spiritualism), the Puerto Rican folk religion. The line of the sun, in palm reading, is the line that crosses the palm of a person's hand; it refers to the mystical nature or the astrological fortune of that person. Spiritualism is a syncretic religion that combines Catholicism and African religious practices. When African slaves were brought to the islands and to much of Latin America, where they provided intensive labor on the sugar-cane plantations, they brought with them the ancient African deities. The Spaniards imposed Catholicism on both the Africans and the indigenous populations. These populations often only superficially adopted Catholicism while still secretly practicing their own religions. Over the years, the syncretism between the two became common. Ortiz Cofer mentions in an interview that most Puerto Ricans saw no conflict between spiritualism and Catholicism: "People on the island believe that *espiritismo* is the same as Catholicism" (Ocasio 46). Ortiz Cofer's own grandfather, like Papá Pepe in the novel, was a *mesa blanca espiritista* who, as Ortiz Cofer recalls in her interview with critic Rafael Ocasio, "only worked through God, not witchcraft" (1). Her grandfather worked with the Bible as well as with a "mahogany stick," which was used to communicate with the dead. Spiritualism today in Puerto Rico may have declined, especially in urban areas, but it is still respected. In New York, one can still find *botánicas,* small shops that sell special herbs (as portrayed in both García's and Hijuelos's novels), and *spiritists.* People from all economic and social backgrounds still seek *spiritists* for guidance and decision making (Kent 25).

According to Ortiz Cofer, religion predominated in her own town of Hormigueros, on which she based the fictitious Salud. She describes the archetypal Puerto Rican woman, including her own mother, as having her "feet on the ground and [her] soul in the church" (Ocasio 46). But Ortiz Cofer parodies the Catholic Church; Padre Gonzalo is tired of his flock, Padre César is run out because he is a homosexual;, and the town is run by the Holy Rosary Society, which is led by two bored housewives, Doña Tina and her friend. These women take it upon themselves to keep the town of Salud free of any perceived bad influences, namely Rosa, *La Cabra.* Rosa, and the valley she lives in, stand outside the town limits of Salud. Symbolically, her individuality and her home represent the "other" in Salud. More than anything else, it is Rosa's indifference to the mores of Catholicism and the strictures of the town of Salud that lead to her persecution.

In Part II of the novel, Ortiz Cofer introduces two *spiritists* in *El Building.* They are Elba, *La Negra* (the Black woman) and *Blanquita* (the White woman). Elba, or *La Negra,* is characterized as a *santera,* whereas *Blanquita* is characterized as *mesa blanca spiritist.* The lines are not clear in distinguishing the two. The narrator defines *santería* as "a sect of spiritists who combined Catholic symbols and ritual with ancient African rites to call forth spirits and to predict and heal. . . . The Mesa Blancas did not have the elaborate paraphernalia of the Santeros but followed the precepts of the European spiritists of the nineteenth century, who needed only a table and a few volunteers to summon spirits" (*Line of the Sun* 238). Unlike *santería,* as seen in García's and Hijuelos's novels, *spiritism* is not seen as dealing in dark forces. *Santería,* according to Ortiz Cofer, is perceived as escapism, whereas *espiritismo* is seen as less of an evil force.

The importance of this folk religion for Puerto Ricans is emphasized by Ortiz Cofer. Both Part I and Part II have *spiritist* meetings, which turn the action of the novel (Bruce Novoa 64). In the first half of the novel, Mamá Cielo seeks help from Rosa. She takes Guzmán to see Rosa for a *despojo* (exorcism), as she believes that Guzmán is possessed by a demon because of his wild behavior. In the second half of the novel, the women of the building prepare a *spiritist* meeting. However, both *spiritist* meetings have the opposite of the desired outcomes. Rosa's *despojo* causes Guzmán to fall in love with Rosa, and the meeting in *El Building* causes the building to burn down. Despite these negative effects, both have positive effects as well. Guzmán and Rosa are the only characters in the novel who do not abide by the strictures of the town and who enjoy true love. The burning down of the building causes Marisol's family to move out of the building in which they have been trapped and allows Gabriel and Marisol to come to terms with their inner realities in a positive way.

In the end, Ortiz Cofer offers a subtle critique of the strictures that characterize both the town of Salud and *El Building*. She sees the insularity and restrictions of both geographical locations as an obstacle to the improvement of Puerto Ricans. In fact, Ortiz Cofer states: "One of my main obsessions and motifs is the island, the isolation of everyone being an island and how isolated you are when you don't know the language. . . . We are trying to re-create island life in a hostile environment" (Kevane and Heredia 117). As long as small towns of fanatical religious devotion do not support characters like Guzmán, and as long as *El Building* restricts the option of acculturation and the constructive integration of Puerto Ricans in the United States, then Puerto Ricans will not succeed. *El Building*, for all of its attempts to mimic the life left behind and to create a sense of security, in many ways limits the members of its community and their possibilities for cultural adaptation. As Ortiz Cofer states, "My main message in my books is that a lifetime is an ongoing process and that evolution doesn't have to always equal progress, but it's inevitable culturally. . . . When kids talk to me about that [being pigeonholed in their identity] I tell them to define themselves and what they feel themselves to be first and then to go back and see what they have adapted from each culture and how much of it they actually need" (Kevane and Heredia 122).

FURTHER SUGGESTED READINGS

Works by Judith Ortiz Cofer

Ortiz Cofer, Judith. *The Meaning of Consuelo.* New York: Farrar, Strauss and Giroux, 2003.

———. *Woman in Front of the Sun: On Becoming a Writer.* Athens: University of Georgia Press, 2000.

———. *The Year of Our Revolution.* Houston: Arte Público Press, 1998.

———. *An Island Like You: Stories of the Barrio.* New York: Orchard Books, 1995.

———. *The Latin Deli: Prose and Poetry.* New York and London: W.W. Norton & Company, 1995.

———. "And Are You a Latina Writer?" Lucha Corpi, Ed. *Máscaras.* Berkeley: Third Woman Press, 1992.

———. *The Line of the Sun.* Athens: University of Georgia Press, 1989.

———. *Silent Dancing: A Partial Remembrance of a Puerto Rican Childhood.* Houston: Arte Público Press, 1990.

———. *Reaching for the Mainland.* Tempe: Bilingual Press, 1987.

———. *Terms of Survival: Poems.* Houston: Arte Público Press, 1987.

———. *Peregrina.* New York: Riverstone, 1986.

———. *Latin Women Pray.* Fort Lauderdale: Florida Arts Gazette Press, 1980.

Other Suggested Fiction

Ferré, Rosario. *Sweet Diamond Dust and Other Stories.* New York: Plume, 1996.

Mohr, Nicholasa. *A Matter of Pride and Other Stories.* Houston: Arte Público Press, 1997.

———. *In My Own Words: Growing Up Inside the Sanctuary of My Imagination.* New York: Simon and Schuster, 1994.

———. *Going Home.* New York: Dial Books for Young Readers, 1986.

———. *Felita.* New York: Dial Press, 1979.

———. *In Nueva York.* New York: Dial Press, 1977.

———. *El Bronx Remembered.* New York: Harper & Row, 1975.

Santiago, Esmeralda. *Almost a Woman.* New York: Random House, 1999.

———. *America's Dream.* New York: HarperCollins, 1996.

———. *When I Was Puerto Rican.* New York: Vintage Books, 1994.

Chapter 8
The Fiction of Ernesto Quiñonez: Bodega Dreams (2000)

Ernesto Quiñonez was born in Ecuador and moved to New York when he was eighteen months old. His father is from Ecuador, his mother from Puerto Rico. Quiñonez's parentage represents what reporter Juan Gonzalez terms the new Latino hybrid, that of Latinos in urban environments who intermarry and interact to create an even more complex culture (174). Quiñonez was raised in East Harlem, which is also called Spanish Harlem, or *El Barrio*, on the upper West Side of Manhattan. He attended the local public school and later studied writing at City College of New York. He published some short stories in *Bomb* magazine that would later be turned into his highly acclaimed first novel *Bodega Dreams* (2000). Quiñonez's novel is a reaction against the concept that Latinos do not read and, thus, literature about them is not necessary. He also wrote this novel for the "thousands of Latinos like me, who either grew up in the United States or were born here" ("Behind the Books" 2). Quiñonez is currently at work on his second novel, while continuing his job as a bilingual fourth-grade teacher in New York.

Quiñonez's goal in writing *Bodega Dreams* was to galvanize Latino readers to action. The author believes that "it is up to ordinary people to bring change because politicians won't" ("Behind the Books" 3). Puerto Ricans on the mainland have been negatively affected by tremendous economic and social forces, racism, poverty, and violence, all of which have taken a toll on them and have stereotyped them as the bottom dwellers of the Latino immigrant hierarchy. Facing these bleak circumstances, Quiñonez wanted to write a novel in which he could demonstrate how young people, in particular, could rise above their circumstances and better themselves ("Behind the Books" 4). The plot of Quiñonez's novel embraces this goal through the mysterious and mythical William Irizarry, or Willie Bodega. Bodega, a former leader of the Young Lords, the radical and political group of Puerto Rican activists that emerged in 1969, dreams of renovating his beloved Spanish Harlem. He wants to transform the depleted geographical and emotional space into a safe and flourishing community.

Bodega seeks to renovate Spanish Harlem through educational means and through business opportunities. He funds college tuition for many in order to create a class of skilled professionals who can become lawyers, doctors, and professors. He also funds small businesses, creating a healthy economy within the community. The only catch, the reader learns, is that in order to fund his community renovation projects, he must traffic in the drug trade. Nevertheless, his final vision is noble: he hopes to create a professional class that can defend and support itself against the American political and social system, a system that denies Puerto Ricans a place, a voice, and the ability to construct a positive image. In addition, with a powerful professional class, *Boricuas* (native Indians of the island, the Tainos, named the island Borinquén; Boricuas means Puerto Ricans) on the mainland will be able to sustain a sense of *orgullo nacional* (national pride) as they see other Puerto Ricans in the media, or working as doctors, lawyers, artists, and more.

Willie Bodega, and the romantic murder-mystery plot in the novel, is strictly fictional, according to Quiñonez. Bodega is modeled on the likes of Jay Gatsby and Kurtz from *Heart of Darkness,* heroes who are also villains, men who see the inevitability of achieving a greater goal through corrupt means. Like many of the novels here, Quiñonez's novel contains autobiographical elements as well: Quiñonez, like Julio "Chino" Mercado, the protagonist of the novel, grew up in *El Barrio,* attended public schools, and fought his classmates in order to attain respect. Also, like Chino, Quiñonez painted "R.I.P.'s" to memorialize people from the neighborhood who had died. In addition, his mother, like the fictional Blanca, is devoutly religious and morally upright, whereas his father was more political and cynical, like Chino.

When asked who served as inspiration for his first novel, Quiñonez mentions the "Nuyorican" writers like Pedro Pietri, Miguel Algarín, and Miguel Piñero. Stanzas from Pietri and Piñero's poems appear in the three parts that divide the novel. The title of the novel also alludes to Piñero's poem, "La Bodega Sold Dreams." *Bodega Dreams,* in this respect, does not only refer to Willie Bodega's dreams of renovating Spanish Harlem, but also to the power of poetry and to the cultural heritage available to new young writers. A *bodega* is a little store with goods from Puerto Rico, Latin American, or the Caribbean in general, that sells items like plantains, black beans, rice, and all the special condiments that are staples of the Latino diet. In addition, a *bodega* is where people gather to *chismear* and *conversar,* to gossip and chat;

to share news of family members left behind on the island, or island politics; to dream of their return to Puerto Rico; of escaping the poverty of the *barrio*, of becoming successful. On the cover and on the inside of the novel are photographs of typical *bodegas* in Spanish Harlem, complete with tropical products and more. The combination of the poems, the utilitarian role of the *bodega*, and the character's dreams combine to suggest the major lesson of the novel: Puerto Ricans should no longer accept empty dreams, but should begin to create change by becoming politically, socially, and economically active.

Chino, the protagonist of *Bodega Dreams*, dramatizes this lesson as he evolves from a character who cannot wait to escape his *barrio* to one who is empowered by his *barrio*. But, Quiñonez did not want to write another autobiographical coming-of-age novel (like the classic *Down These Mean Streets* by Piri Thomas) only. He dedicates one small chapter to the young Chino and then moves quickly into the high drama. In this way, Quiñonez has more room to explore the larger themes that plague the *barrio*, not just those of one individual. A central question that Quiñonez wanted to address in his novel reveals his own social consciousness and obsessions: "Why is it that we keep failing the residents of inner city ghettos? . . . Someone has to change things" ("Behind the Books" 3). Chino's transformation remains collective in that it rests on a vision of a new race of Puerto Ricans on the mainland.

Bodega Dreams has been well received by critics and readers alike. Young Latino readers embrace this novel and are proud of the fact that it celebrates the customs of their people—hanging out on stoops after dark, chatting, listening to salsa in the streets, and *chismeando* (gossiping). (Readers can find reviews of the novel on line at Amazon.com, which include student comments.) Critics have praised it as well, some lauding Quiñonez for stressing the importance of Spanglish as a fundamental element of Puerto Rican Spanish Harlem, and of the culture of *Boricuas* on the mainland. Others have noted that the mystery/detective/love story works well, as it immediately engages readers and allows Quiñonez the opportunity to reveal his vision for Spanish Harlem.

Bodega Dreams (2000)

The novel, divided into three parts, is narrated in the first person by the protagonist, Julio "Chino" Mercado, who tells Willie Bodega's story while contemplating the past. The time frame is unspecified, yet it is clear that it is a contemporary setting roughly three decades after the advent of the Young Lords and the Civil Rights movement. The action transpires in less than a year, following Blanca's pregnancy from the end of her first trimester until her last trimester, but before she gives birth. The story of Willie

Bodega affects Chino in a dramatic fashion. Before Chino meets Bodega, he wants nothing more than to leave everything behind, to shed his past, and to create a new self. By the end, however, he realizes that he cannot shed his past, and that he can refashion a new identity with the elements that characterize his past in *El Barrio*.

The titles of each part of the novel—Book I, "Because Men Who Built This Country Were Men from the Streets," Book II, "Because a Single Lawyer Can Steal More Money Than a Hundred Men with Guns," and Book III, "A New Language Being Born"—reflect a toying by the author with fundamental concepts on which the United States is based. The men who built *this* country, Spanish Harlem, were men from the streets (not the founding fathers), and because Spanish Harlem has been cheated by politicians, a new language must be born. The novel functions around this idea as the protagonist ends the narration with his vision and understanding of a new Spanish Harlem. Book III, in fact, serves as a manifesto, a call to arms, for future generations. The chapters of each book are subtitled Round 1, Round 2, and so on, and the last chapter of each book is subtitled Knockout. Quiñonez creates a parallel between the narration and a boxing match, emphasizing the struggle and difficulty that young Puerto Ricans face when trying to emerge successfully from their environment, when trying to achieve a better level of social awareness, effectiveness, and improved social standing.

Book I opens with a stanza from the "Nuyorican" poet Pedro Pietri's poem "Puerto Rican Obituary." The stanza plays on the theme of hopeless dreams and false promises that characterize the lives of inner-city Puerto Ricans: "All died/hating the grocery stores/that sold them make-believe steak and bullet-proof rice/and beans/All died waiting dreaming and hating." The *bodega* appears again but this time, instead of participating in the illusions and dreams of the people who gather at the *bodega*, the poet criticizes the fake commodities found in the store and how they paralyze, with hatred, the members of the community.

Book I contains nine chapters that describe Julio's beginnings, following him from junior high school to his marriage to Blanca, who is a member of the Pentecostal Church. They enroll in Hunter College as a path to success and an escape from the *barrio*. Although the novel is not, as Quiñonez stated, a coming-of-age novel, identity is important. The first chapter of the novel reveals the kind of identity one achieves with one's peers.

The first chapter is perhaps the most important chapter of the novel since it describes the environment, the loss of hope, the obstacles, and the poverty that characterize the neighborhood. Julio lives in a *barrio* where "Fires, junkies, dying, shootouts, holdups, babies falling out of windows were things you took as part of life" (*Bodega* 5). The collective sense of self-worth for most of the young Puerto Ricans is that of self-hatred; life "meant shit. . . . You lived in projects with pissed-up elevators, junkies on the stairs, posters of the rapist of the month" (*Bodega* 4–5). Survival depends on a system of codes, mostly unfamiliar to those outside of Spanish Harlem. In order to earn respect, one must engage in violence. Participating in this violence is easy, according to Julio, because of a collective lack of self-respect. The Puerto Rican *barrio* youth internalize a great deal of self-hatred, which promotes the idea that there is nothing to lose in fighting and possibly dying. In fact, by fighting one stands the chance of gaining respect. According to Julio, if you fight enough you earn a nickname, and that means status: "You were somebody. If anyone called you by your real name [the name given to you by your parents] you were *un mamao,* a useless, meaningless thing" (*Bodega* 4). Julio, although not naturally violent, wants to achieve a sense of self, like his best friend Enrique, whose nickname is Sapo (Toad). Julio is beaten and beats others every day at school until he is granted the nickname of Chino, which means "you looked a bit Chinese, and second, you had to fight. It was an honor to be called Chino" (*Bodega* 8). As with Esperanza in Cisneros's novel *The House on Mango Street,* with Chino, Quiñonez plays on the significance of names, of wanting a new name from which one, as a young individual can derive a sense of self-worth. Unlike his best friend Sapo, all Chino wants is to leave Spanish Harlem (again, like Esperanza). Sapo, on the other hand, loves and is proud of his "homeland," his *barrio.* He asks Chino why he would ever want to leave the *barrio,* saying, "This neighborhood is beautiful, bro" (*Bodega* 11). Chino thinks he knows the answer to Sapo's question. But, it is not until he meets Bodega that the question posed by Sapo will be resolved.

After the first chapter, the plot shifts to Chino's encounter with Willie Bodega. The second chapter begins with Chino's first trip outside the parameters of his *barrio.* He is accepted into the High School of Art and Design on 57th Street, and "without my quite knowing it, the world became new" (*Bodega* 12). During his last year at the high school, Chino learns about Futurist artists and the idea that cultures die and are in constant need of reinvention. Chino's attraction to the Futurists centers on the idea of abandoning one's past and identity: "I realized that by reinventing culture, they were reinventing themselves. I wanted to reinvent myself too. I no longer wanted the world to be just my neighborhood anymore" (*Bodega* 13). Chino and his future wife Blanca enroll in Hunter College, knowing that education can lead to change.

Although Blanca and Chino are committed to change and self-betterment through education, the idea that change can be accomplished through legitimate means is questioned when they meet Bodega. Bodega accomplishes change through the negative and destructive channels of the drug trade. Chino comes to acknowledge and accept this as a temporary means to an end. He does not judge Bodega's darker side, but rather the side that maintains positive ideals for his community. When Quiñonez was asked if he worried about the perception that he was advocating drug money, Quiñonez responded: "Readers who say I'm glorifying a drug dealer may be the same readers who overlook how much Gatsby [Jay Gatsby] was romanticized by Fitzgerald. Like Gatsby, Bodega has broken the law; the difference is that Bodega is also renovating buildings, helping the community" ("Behind the Books" 2).

Willie Bodega, although technically a drug trafficker and a villain, simultaneously represents all the dreams of ideal young Puerto Ricans. Initially, however, Chino remains blind to the historical and social knowledge that Bodega possesses. He pokes fun at Bodega, stating that he is a relic of the olden days, an individual out of touch with reality. In fact, however, as we learn along with Chino, he is quite the opposite. Bodega knows about Puerto Rican contributions to the United States, knows that they are perceived as third-class citizens, and knows that they are not going to receive respect unless they create it. Chino does not see this at the time he meets Bodega but, because he is narrating a story that has already taken place, he lets us know how wrong he was to perceive Bodega as a joke. He will come to realize how important people like Bodega are to the survival and to *la dignidad* (the dignity) of Puerto Ricans in East Harlem. When Bodega talks about his dream for a Puerto Rican Great Society, Chino laughs: "Who did he think he was, Lyndon Johnson? Back then, that night, to me he was a joke. . . . I was to discover that I was living in a rare moment when a personality becomes so interlocked with the ear that it can't be spoken of in different sentences. Bodega was a lost relic from a time when all things seemed possible. When young people cared about social change" (*Bodega* 30). Slowly Chino becomes enamored of Willie Bodega, to the degree that he begins to invent Bodega's past: "I pictured Bodega back in those days so young, flying with invisible wings. Thinking that freeing an island from U.S. control could be done with passion and intellect. . . . Her [Vera's] liberator, who was first going to free her from her mother, then free Puerto Rico, and later they would both sail back to America like conquistadors in reverse. They would arrive in New York Harbor and Latinos from all five boroughs would be there to greet them" (*Bodega* 125).

Book II contains twelve chapters that further embroil Chino in Bodega's schemes. It contains both the climax and denouement of the novel. The second book opens with another stanza from Pedro Pietri's "Puerto Rican Obituary": "These dreams/These empty dreams/from the make-believe bedrooms/their parents left them." At this point, Chino considers Bodega a combination of "nobility and street, as if God never made up his mind whether to have Bodega be born a leader or a hood" (*Bodega* 85). This part of the novel reunites Bodega with Vera, his long-lost love, only to end in disaster when both Nazario, Bodega's lawyer, and Vera betray the noble Bodega and kill him. As Chino becomes more involved with Bodega, at the risk of his own marriage with Blanca, he begins to believe in the ideals and dreams that define Bodega's purpose in life. But Bodega's dreams for renovation are side-tracked by Vera, who happens to be Blanca's aunt. Vera had left *El Barrio* to marry a wealthy Cuban in Miami. Bodega and Vera had known each other from their days with the Young Lords, but Vera had abandoned Willie, saying that he lacked vision. Bodega, believing this and hoping to impress her with his new wealth and godfather-like status in the *barrio*, assigns Chino the role of finding Vera and bringing her back to Spanish Harlem. Bodega believes that once Vera witnesses his success, she will marry him. Initially, Vera agrees and appears to be in love with Bodega. Chino, like the reader, believes Vera. The second book ends with the discovery that Vera is not really in love with Bodega, but rather with Bodega's lawyer, Nazario. In the end, Willie Bodega is betrayed not only by Vera and Nazario, but also by his own ideals and trust, by the hopes and dreams that he still harbors from his days as an activist in the Young Lords Party.

Book III opens with a stanza from Miguel Piñero's poem "La Bodega Sold Dreams." "dreamt I was this poeta/words glitterin' brite & bold/in las bodegas/where our poets' words & songs/are sung." The songs of the *bodega*, the poetry that emerges from the people who gather there, can and should have more impact than the products sold there. Words are transformed into the "brite & bold" products found in the *bodega*. The *poeta* (poet) serves as the soothsayer, predicting the future of his people. Bodega was, in some respects, a poet full of dreams and ideals and the ability to act on them. In the end, tragically, Bodega is betrayed not because he cannot fulfill his promises, but because noble people like Bodega cannot survive. The subtitle for Book III, "Pa'lante, Siempre Pa'lante," a contraction for *para adelante*, or moving forward, always forward, is a typical expression both on the island and in *El Barrio*. It encourages people in the daily struggle of survival. The Young Lords Party, in fact, published a newspaper called *Palante* (Luis 44).

Book III has only one chapter, the eulogy, which, like the title, serves multiple purposes. It stands as a funeral oration in praise of Willie Bodega, who is respected and admired for his contributions to the community, for his ideals, for the fact that he helped Puerto Ricans help themselves, and for his belief that Spanish Harlem is a legitimate space of beauty and power. At Bodega's funeral, the "Spanish Harlem aristocracy" appear and have cameo roles. They are the Young Lords and the "Nuyorican" poets and writers. Quiñonez introduces actual members of the Puerto Rican community in Spanish Harlem into his fictional novel. These politicians and writers, as Julio notes, form the cornerstone of both the roots and the branches of the *barrio*, of the past and future. They are the real dreamers, the real people who fought for change in Spanish Harlem, the original Young Lord activists, and the founders and participants of the Nuyorican Poets' Café poetry group.

The eulogy celebrates Spanish Harlem and the possibilities of creating a new race and a new language. Julio's final vision appears to him in a dream about Bodega. In the dream, Bodega and Julio see a woman yelling out of the window to her son: "*Mira*, Junito, go buy *un mapo, un contén de leche*, and tell *el bodeguero yo le pago* next Friday. And I don't want to see you in *el rufo!* [Listen, Junito, go buy a mop, a carton of milk, and tell the grocery man that I will pay him next Friday. And I don't want to see you in the roof; my translation]" (*Bodega* 212). Bodega and Julio observe this scene together, and then Bodega tells Julio: "You know what is happening here, don't you? Don't you? What we just heard was a poem, Chino. It's a beautiful new language. Don't you see what's happening? A new language means a new race. Spanglish is the future. It's a new language being born out of the ashes of two cultures clashing with each other" (*Bodega* 212).

CULTURAL ELEMENTS

The unique aspect of *Bodega Dreams* is the celebration of Spanish Harlem as the Puerto Rican homeland on the mainland. Quiñonez advocates for Puerto Ricans in Manhattan to maintain a stake in their *barrio,* to derive *orgullo* from *El Barrio* by learning about its past and working toward its future. Although thought of by the dominant culture as poor, dangerous, and inconsequential, Spanish Harlem has a rich culture filled with political activists, poets, writers, musicians, unique religious practices, and dreams and ideals. Because Julio's generation, including his wife and their unborn child, retain little connection to the island of Puerto Rico, they should foster a stronger relationship to Spanish Harlem. In this regard, it is important to note that Quiñonez "codifies" Spanish Harlem, as critic Ed Morales points out, not only giving us an historical background, but also addressing the Spanglish that characterizes the community: "The most ingenious thing about *Bodega Dreams* is the way it codifies much of the East Harlem experience, with its Young Lords legends, Santeria rituals, and bilingual bards. Like Junot Diaz and Abraham Rodriguez, Quiñonez is helping to establish Spanglish as a new-millennium urban language" (1).

Bodega Dreams serves as testimony to the historical and cultural participation of Puerto Ricans on the mainland. Quiñonez highlights the rich history and culture present in Spanish Harlem by resurrecting and paying tribute to several mainland-born Puerto Rican cultural phenomena: the Young Lords Party, the arts and literary community as seen through Taller Boricua, the Nuyorican Poets' Café, graffiti mural art, and the Salsa Museum. The Young Lords emerged in 1969 in response to the "mistrust and misunderstanding" of Puerto Ricans on the mainland (Gonzalez 93). Quiñonez clearly did his research on the Young Lords. Julio describes them accurately and with great historical detail as a revolutionary group that wrote the important "Thirteen Point Program and Platform," listing their priorities, from freeing Puerto Rico from the U.S. to helping the neighborhoods.

Despite the fact that Puerto Ricans are American citizens, and have been since 1917 and passage of the Jones Act, despite the fact that they have lived on the mainland for over a century and that they have participated in every major war since World War II, they have remained marginal to the dominant culture. They have been treated not only as third-class citizens, but also as foreign immigrants, never truly being considered American citizens. The Young Lords (along with many radical political groups that arose out of the Civil Rights movement) sought to galvanize Latinos in politics and to bring attention to the history of Puerto Ricans and their contributions to the United States. Quiñonez pays tribute to the Young Lords because he wants Latinos to have a connection with their past, to recognize the vital role political activist groups can play in shaping the future and in creating collective and individual empowerment.

At Bodega's funeral, Quiñonez includes cameo appearances of not only former Young Lords members, but also of poets, writers, and artists from the "Nuyorican" literary and artistic scene. (Many Young Lords activists were also poets, like Pedro Pietri.) Members of Taller Boricua, who make an appearance, are part of an almost thirty-year-old visual arts organization in Spanish Harlem. It helps artists display their work, and it gives students in public schools and shelters art classes. Poets from the Nuyorican Poets' Café, founded in the seventies by Miguel Algarín, make an appearance as well: Sandra Maria Esteves, Pedro Pietri, and even Miguel Piñero, who died in 1988. Quiñonez includes novelists fundamental to the "Nuyorican" literary tradition like Piri Thomas (*Down These Mean Streets*), Edward Rivera (*Family Installments*), and Jack Agüeros (*Dominoes and Other Short Stories*). Both Taller Boricua and the Poets' Café remain a central forum for budding poets, writers, and artists with strong ties to the Spanish Harlem community. In addition, Quiñonez pays special attention to Julia de Burgos (1914–1953), one of Puerto Rico's most famous poets, who died forgotten in a hospital in Harlem and was buried anonymously. Although Chino's public school is named Julia de Burgos Junior High School 99 (also known as Jailhouse 99), Chino knows nothing about her. When he discovers what an important poet she was in Puerto Rico, he wonders why no one taught her work in class. He questions why Latino students are consistently taught more about Italy and Robert Frost than they are about their own cultural roots and heritage (*Bodega* 6).

Quiñonez pays tribute to the Salsa Museum, which houses the history of salsa music—an *afro-jíbario-antillano* music, as the protagonist calls it— along with all the big names in music, Tito Puente, Willie Colón, Hector Lavoe, and more. According to William Luis, "Salsa is a New York phenomenon, born of urban culture, of the marginal Hispanic and Latino community. . . . it speaks to the pains, problems, and ailments of the Latino community in New York" (211). Willie Colón and Hector Lavoe exemplify salsa musicians who employed music as social protest. Together, Colón and

Lavoe sang about the difficulties Puerto Ricans and many Latinos face on the mainland. When Julio enters the Salsa Museum, he feels like he is returning to an earlier time, when there was hope for the future of Puerto Ricans on the mainland. Lastly, Quiñonez includes a brief, though important, scene of the "graffiti hall of fame," public artistic murals that color Spanish Harlem. In his dream at the end of the novel, Julio sees graffiti murals that include Bodega along with the other important Latino greats: "Zapata, Albizu Campos, Sandino, Martí, and Malcolm, along with a million Adelitas" (*Bodega* 213). Quiñonez highlights a cosmic race of famous men that includes blacks and women, along with well-known Latin American figures: Emiliano Zapata and the Adelitas; female revolutionary soldiers from the Mexican Revolution; Pedro Albizu Campos, an important political activist who fought for Puerto Rican independence; Augusto Sandino, who fought for Nicaraguan independence; Jose Martí, the great Cuban poet and freedom fighter; and Malcolm X, one of the most important figures from the Civil Rights Movement.

Quiñonez also pays tribute to these institutions and to their respective members because, as he says in an interview, he wanted to "make sure that they will not be forgotten outside of the Latino community. They are part of our national lore, just like American cowboys" ("Behind the Books" 2). In addition, Quiñonez, through this novel, expresses the belief that alliances among different groups can help accomplish the dream of a reenergized Spanish Harlem. All of these forms of political and artistic expression emerged from a sense of outrage and social protest. Thus, Quiñonez, along with the figures to whom he pays tribute, are using political and artistic forums to protest the perception of Puerto Ricans and Latinos as part of a marginal society.

The inclusion of these cultural institutions and forms of artistic expression rooted in Spanish Harlem, of important political and artistic members of the community, and of Puerto Rican culture, also emphasizes Quiñonez's belief that a lack of knowledge about one's cultural heritage contributes to a collective self-hatred. Quiñonez not only criticizes his peers, but also the public school system and the media. They are institutions that control what Latinos learn, their self-perception, and the public's perception of them. Established newspapers, according to Chino, ignore all Hispanic issues. Quiñonez denounces the public school system and newspapers for perpetuating the myth that there is nothing of worth in Puerto Rican or Latino culture and, therefore, nothing to teach or to report. In the public schools, Julio notices that his fellow students collectively believe they had no culture to celebrate. Quiñonez, like Junot Díaz and Sandra Cisneros, points to public-school teachers as people who directly impact, shape, and form students, influencing their self-esteem and sense of self-worth. The teachers in the schools "demonize" the students, to use Junot Díaz's term. Public schools should criticize the lack of funding from the state and federal governments.

As the narrators states, In turn, the young Hispanic teachers work at countering this, at building the students' self-esteem, which they believe is more important than standardized tests.

Gender roles are also addressed within the new vision for Spanish Harlem, although they do not take center stage. However, Quiñonez has stated that his next novel will address fundamental customs like sexism and machismo because they affect women: "Women have to be given more power, and some laws and cultural customs will have to change, machismo will have to be obliterated" ("Behind the Books" 2). Many of the characters surrounding Chino and Blanca are stereotypical—Sapo, for instance, who dreams of becoming the next drug lord, and Blanca's sister Negra, who is a victim of domestic abuse, is unemployed, and is frozen in a gender role assigned to her by the patriarchal system typical of Latino societies. Chino and Blanca, along with their unborn child, however, represent a new family that might also make Spanish Harlem a vital and important space.

Blanca is a Puerto Rican woman who has avoided the trappings of the *barrio*—violence, drugs, teenage pregnancy—and is on her way to attaining success. In many ways, Blanca attributes her success to her Pentecostal church, which keeps watch over its members, and whose pastor was once a drug addict and speaks from experience. Unlike Julio, she avoids using the *barrio* nicknames and avoids participating in or acknowledging the drug dealing and violence. Julio, although temporarily sidetracked, represents a new Latino man. Julio cooks dinner, is not threatened by his wife's intelligence or education, allows her to pursue her dreams, and states that, unlike the typical macho Latino man, he has no desire to prove his virility by cheating on his wife. That their child will be born after Chino's transformation augurs well for the new generation of young Puerto Ricans that Bodega dreams of in the novel. Theirs will be a child with a strong sense of pride, a knowledge of his or her cultural heritage, and the ability to escape the trappings of the Latin patriarchal system. The novel ends with the impending birth of Julio and Blanca's child, and also with the arrival of a new immigrant family, an older man and a small boy. Julio, who encounters them on the street, momentarily turns away, only to return and to offer them his home as a temporary haven. In this way, Julio continues Bodega's dreams of helping new immigrants and the community as a whole.

Absent from *Bodega Dreams* is that *añoranza*, that longing for the homeland. The island of Puerto Rico is no longer a significant presence for this generation. Although the action takes place within one generation, the idea behind the novel is that there are generations of roots, of Puerto Ricans in East Harlem, who claim this space as their home. In this respect, unlike many of the other novels in this book, we are only shown how it is now for young Puerto Ricans in the United States. The parents of the characters are not present in the novel, and the homeland is not depicted like it is in *The Line of the Sun* or in Alvarez's novels. Harlem is where several generations of Puerto Ricans have been born. Harlem stands as the homeland that some adore, like Sapo, and that some hate, like Vera. Harlem needs to be taken care of. As Quiñonez states in his novel, many landlords were burning down buildings and benefiting from it. Whole blocks, the narrator says, would disappear. Bodega, in the novel, buys the dilapidated buildings, and literally gentrifies his own neighborhood, turning it into a community homeland from which Puerto Ricans can derive pride. But, if the idea of return exists in this novel, it takes place on the mainland, not with Puerto Rico. Those who leave the *barrio,* like Vera, want to return to the *barrio* to gloat. They do not want to return to the island.

In the end, Quiñonez's novel takes a social stand. It links past and present as a call to arms to the next generations. Spanish Harlem, *El Barrio,* becomes one of the most important characters in the novel in that the characters must contend with, learn about, and take care of it in order to be a successful community in the United States. In this sense, Quiñonez's novel stands as a social treatise that urges his fellow Puerto Ricans to better themselves by taking pride in their homeland in the United States.

FURTHER SUGGESTED READINGS

"Behind the Books: Author Q & A's" Interview with Ernesto Quiñonez. <http://www.randomhouse.com/vintage>, Fall 2002.

Luis, William. *Dance Between Two Cultures: Latino Caribbean Literature Written in the United States.* Nashville and London: Vanderbilt University Press, 1997.

Morales, Ed. "Review of *Bodega Dreams*" <http://www.barnesandnoble.com/booksearch/htp>, Fall 2002.

Pietri, Pedro. *Puerto Rican Obituary.* New York: Monthly Review Press, 1974.

Rivera, Edward. *Family Installments: Memories of Growing Up Hispanic.* New York: Penguin Group, 1983.

Rodriguez, Abraham Jr. *Spidertown* (2d ed.). New York: Penguin USA, 1994.

Thomas, Piri. *Down These Mean Streets.* 1967. New York: Vintage Books, 1991.

Selected Bibliography

A Selected Bibliography of Useful Background and Critical Texts

Abalos, David T. *La Comunidad Latina in the United States: Person and Political Strategies for Tranforming Culture*. Westport, CT: Praeger, 1998.

Anaya, Rudolfo. "The Writer's Landscape: Epiphany in Landscape." *Latin American Review* 5:10 (Spring-Summer 1978): 98–102.

———. "La Llorona, El Kookooee, and Sexuality." *The Bilingual Review/La revista bilingüe* 17: 1 (1992): 50–55.

Anaya, Rudolfo, and Francisco Lomeli, eds. *Aztlán: Essays on the Chicano Homeland*. Albuquerque: University of New Mexico Press, 1991.

Augenbraum, Harold, and Stavans, Ilan, eds. *Growing Up Latino: Memoirs and Stories*. Boston and New York: Houghton Mifflin, 1993.

Bandon, Alexandra. *Dominican Americans*. Parsippany: New Discovery Books, 1995.

"Behind the Books: Author Q & A's." Interview with Ernesto Quinonez. <http://www.randomhouse.com/vintage>, 1.

Bruce-Novoa, Juan. "Ritual in Judith Ortiz Cofer's *The Line of the Sun*" in *Confluencia* 8:1 (Fall 1993): 61–69.

———. "Hijuelos' *Mambo Kings:* Reading from Divergent Traditions." *Confluencia* 10:2 (Spring 1995): 11–22.

Calderón, Héctor. " 'Como Mexico No Hay Dos': Sandra Cisneros's Feminist Border Stories." *Narratives of Greater Mexico: Essays on Chicano Literary History, Genre and Borders*. Austin: University of Texas Press (2004).

———. "To Read Chicano Narrative: Commentary and Metacommentary." *Mester* 11:2 (1983): 3–13.

Céspedes, Diógenes, and Silvio Torres-Saillant. "Fiction Is the Poor Man's Cinema: An Interview with Junot Díaz." <http://www.callaloo.com>. JHU Press. 23: 3 (2000): 892–907.

"Christian Legends in Cisneros' Work." Cisneros' Goody Bag of Myths and Legends. <geocities.com/SoHo/Workshop/4911/wgww/sandra/myths. html> 2.

Coerver, Don, and Linda Hall, eds. *Tangled Destinies: Latin America and the United States*. Albuquerque: The University of New Mexico Press, 1999.

"Crucible of Empire." War of 1898 Interactive Web Center. <http://pbs.org>

Dash, Robert C., et al. "*Bless Me, Ultima* at Twenty-Five Years: A Conversation with Rudolfo Anaya." *Americas Review* 25 (1999): 150–163.

de Jesús, Joy L., ed. *Growing Up Puerto Rican: An Anthology*. New York: Avon Books, 1997.

Esdaille, Milca. "Same Trip, Different Ships." *Black Issues Book Review* 3:2 (March 2001): 40.

Flores, Juan. *From Bomba to Hip-Hop*. New York: Columbia University Press, 2000.

"Giving His People a Voice (information about the life of author Junot Díaz)." *People Weekly* 47:1 (13 Jan. 1997): 77.

Gonzalez, Juan. *Harvest of Empire: A History of Latinos in America*. New York: Viking, 2000.

The Guadalupe: Patroness of the Americas. <www.loveandmercy.org> 1.

Jacklosky, Rob. "*Drown*: Book Review." *Studies in Short Fiction* 35:1 (Winter 1998): 93.

Kallet, Marilyn, and Judith Ortiz Cofer, eds. *Sleeping with One Eye Open*. Athens and London: University of Georgia Press, 1999.

Kanellos, Nicolás. *Hispanic American Literature: A Brief Introduction and Anthology*. Berkeley: HarperCollins Literary Mosaic, 1995.

Kevane, Bridget and Juanita Heredia, eds. *Latina Self-Portraits: Interviews with Contemporary Women Writers*. Albuquerque: University of New Mexico Press, 2000.

Kent, Deborah. *Puerto Rico*. Chicago: Children's Press, 1992.

Knight, Franklin W. *The Caribbean: The Genesis of a Fragmented Nationalism*. New York: Oxford University Press, 1990.

Lewis, L.M. "Ethnic and Gender Identity: Parallel Growth in Sandra Cisneros' *Woman Hollering Creek*." *Short Story* 2:2 (1994): 69–78.

Luis, William. *Dance between Two Cultures: Latino Caribbean Literature Written in the United States*. Nashville and London: Vanderbilt University Press, 1997.

Martínez, Oscar J. *Mexican-Origin People in the United States: A Topical History*. Tucson: University of Arizona Press, 2001.

McCracken, Ellen. *New Latina Narrative: The Feminine Space of Postmodern Ethnicity*. Tucson: University of Arizona Press, 1999.

Morales Carrión, Arturo. *Puerto Rico: A Political and Cultural History*. New York: W.W. Norton & Co., 1983.

Moya Pons, Frank. *The Dominican Republic: A National History*. Princeton: Markus Wiener Publishers, 1998.

Novas, Himilce. *Everything You Need to Know about Latino History*. New York and London: Plume, 1994.

Ocasio, Rafael. "Puerto Rican Literature in Georgia?: Interview with Judith Ortiz Cofer." *The Kenyon Review* 14.4 (Fall 1992): 43–50.

Ortiz Cofer, Judith."Hers." *Glamour Magazine* (January 1992): 136.

Paravisini-Gebert, Lizabeth. "Junot Díaz's *Drown:* Revisiting 'Those Mean Streets.' " *U.S. Latino Literature: A Critical Guide for Students & Teachers.* Westport: Greenwood Press, 2000.

Parkes, Henry Bamford. *A History of Mexico.* Boston: Houghton Mifflin Co., 1960.

Payant, Katherine. "Borderland Themes in Sandra Cisneros's *Woman Hollering Creek.*" *The Immigrant Experience in North American Literature: Carving Out a Niche.* Ed. Katherine Payant and Toby Rose. Westport and London: Greenwood Press, 1999. 95–109.

Pérez Firmat, Gustavo. *Life on the Hyphen: The Cuban-American Way.* Austin: University of Texas Press, 1994.

Pérez, Jr., Louis A. *Cuba: Between Reform and Revolution.* New York and Oxford: Oxford University Press, 1995.

Poey, Delia, and Suarez, Virgil, eds. *Iguana Dreams.* New York: Harper Perennial, 1992.

Rebolledo, Tey Diana. *Women Singing in the Snow: A Cultural Analysis of Chicana Literature.* Tucson and London: University of Arizona Press, 1995.

Rivera, Jenny. "Domestic Violence against Latinas by Latino Males." *The Latino Condition: A Critical Reader.* Ed. Richard Delgado and Jean Stefancic. New York and London: New York University Press, 1998. 501–507.

Rogozinski, Jan. *A Brief History of the Caribbean: From the Arawak and Carib to the Present.* New York and London: Plume, 2000.

Roorda, Eric Paul. *The Dictator Next Door: The Good Neighbor Policy and the Trujillo Regime in the Dominican Republic, 1930–1945 (American Encounters/ Global Interactions).* Durham and London: Duke University Press, 1998.

Roy, Maya. *Cuban Music.* Trans. Denise Asfar and Gabriel Asfar. Princeton: Markus Wiener Publishers, 2002.

Sagás, Ernesto, and Inoa, Orlando, eds.*The Dominican People: A Documentary History.* Princeton: Markus Wiener Publishers, 2003.

Sanchez Gonzalez, Lisa. *Boricua Literature: A Literary History of the Puerto Rican Diaspora.* New York: New York University Press, 2001.

Sánchez, George J. *Becoming Mexican American: Ethnicity, Culture and Identity in Chicano Los Angeles, 1900–1945.* New York and Oxford: Oxford University Press, 1993.

Sánchez, Luis Rafael. "La guagua aerea." Trans. Diana Vélez. *Village Voice.* January 24, 1984.

Santiago, Roberto, ed. *Boricuas: Influential Puerto Rican Writings—An Anthology.* New York: Ballantine, 1995.

Sirias, Silvio, and Bruce Dick, eds. *Conversations with Rudolfo Anaya.* Literary Conversations Series. Jackson: University Press of Mississippi, 1998.

Smithsonian Institution's U.S. Latino History & Culture. <http://www.si.edu/ resource/faq/nmah/latino.html>

Stavans, Ilan. *The Hispanic Condition: Reflections on Culture & Identity in America.* New York: HarperCollins, 1995.

Suárez-Orozco, Marcelo M., and Mariela Paéz, eds. *Latinos: Remaking America.* Berkeley, Los Angeles, and London: University of California Press, 2002.

Suchlicki, Jaime. *Cuba: From Columbus to Castro and Beyond.* Dulles: Brasseys, Inc., 2002.

Szulc, Tad. *Fidel: A Critical Portrait.* New York: Perennial, 2000.

Torre, Carlos Antonio, Hugo Rodríguez Vecchini, and William Burgos, eds. *The Commuter Nation: Perspectives on Puerto Rican Migration.* San Juan: Editorial de La Universidad de Puerto Rico, 1994.

Turner, Faythe, ed. *Puerto Rican Writers at Home in the USA: An Anthology.* Seattle: Open Hand Publishing, 1991.

Vasquez, Emilia. "Thoughts on 'Fiesta' and 'The Sun, The Moon, The Stars.' " <http://www.ccc.commnet.edu/latinoguide/secondary/Junot_Diaz. html>.

Vasquez, Francisco H., and Rudolfo D. Torres, eds. *Latino/a Thought: Culture, Politics, and Society.* New York and Oxford: Rowman & Littlefield, Inc., 2002.

Vassallo, Paul, ed. "In Commemoration: *One Million Volumes.*" *The Magic of Words: Rudolfo A. Anaya and His Writings.* Albuquerque: University of New Mexico Press, 1982.

Womack, John. *Zapata and the Mexican Revolution.* New York: Random House, 1970.

Zakrzewski Brown, Isabel. *Culture and Customs of the Dominican Republic.* Culture and Customs of Latin America and the Caribbean Series. Westport and London: Greenwood Press, 1999.

Zeledón, Maximo. "Dominican Dominion" <http://www.fronteramag.com/ issue5/Diaz/index.htm>, April 8, 2002.

Websites

García and Holmes http://web.nmsu.edu/~tomlynch/swlit.anaya.html

La Frontera history http://www.pbs.org/kpbs/theborder/

Index

ABOUT THE AUTHOR

BRIDGET KEVANE is Associate Professor of Spanish at Montana State University, Bozeman.

810.9   Kevane, Bridget A.,
Kev   1963-

         Latino literature in
         America.